W9-AEG-968

CATCHING UP WITH THE CHURCH

BX 1754
.O16

CATCHING UP
WITH
THE CHURCH

Catholic Faith and Practice Today

JOHN A. O'BRIEN

KANSAS SCHOOL OF RELIGION
UNIVERSITY OF KANSAS
1300 OREAD AVENUE
LAWRENCE, KANSAS 66044

HERDER AND HERDER

1967
HERDER AND HERDER NEW YORK
232 Madison Avenue, New York 10016

Nihil obstat: Brendan W. Lawlor, Censor Librorum
Imprimatur: ✝ Robert F. Joyce, Bishop of Burlington
February 17, 1967

Catholic church — doctrines
Vatican Council — 2nd

Library of Congress Catalog Card Number: 67-18559
© 1967 by John A. O'Brien
Manufactured in the United States

Do they want the Church to go back to infancy? They forget that Jesus has compared the Kingdom of heaven to a little seed that must grow and develop into a mighty tree.

Pope Paul VI

TO

MR. AND MRS. W. CLEMENT STONE,
IN TOKEN OF GRATITUDE,
FRIENDSHIP AND AFFECTION,
THE AUTHOR DEDICATES THIS WORK

CONTENTS

PREFACE

BY RICHARD CARDINAL CUSHING

VATICAN Council II will doubtless go down in history as the greatest religious event of the twentieth century. From every country prelates, theologians and Scripture scholars converged upon Rome and assembled in St. Peter's, the historic center of Christendom. There they were joined by noted theologians and scholars of other faiths, acting as observers for their respective Churches.

In four lengthy sessions from 1962 to 1966 the Council focused its attention upon the renewal of the Church's interior life, the increasing of the relevance of its teachings for the modern world and the achievement of Christian unity. Of such profound and far-reaching importance were its deliberations that virtually every phase of Catholic life and thought has been vitally affected.

If the decrees, declarations and constitutions of the Council are to be properly implemented and to bear abundant fruit, they must be carried not only to seminaries, universities and colleges but also to the rank and file of Catholics in every land. Their impact upon Christian faith and practice must be clearly set forth for all Christians to see.

This is precisely what *Catching Up With the Church* does in a scholarly and lucid manner. Here one finds the fresh and arresting insights of Vatican Council II, which will vitalize and enrich his religious life. Hence the volume meets a keenly felt need on the part not only of Catholics but also of all Christians concerned with the achievements of that unity for which Christ prayed. Clear, scholarly and up-to-date, *Catching Up With the Church* merits millions of readers.

FOREWORD

BY LOUIS BOUYER

We are in an epoch of great change both in the world and in the Church. This creates inevitably a feeling of crisis. Within the Church some people are startled to see changes in so many matters which they had supposed to be unchangeable. Others seem to imagine that, since so much has changed in such little time, everything else is also to be altered. This situation has engendered fear and dismay among some; others it has spurred to attempt revolution where only a renewal was intended. Is it any wonder that so many people are experiencing uncertainty, misgiving and even panic? Obviously we need to separate the chaff from the wheat, to determine what is to be renewed and what is to remain immutable.

The reader will find this book written with sprightliness and verve, interesting and gripping and yet sound and scholarly. It will engender in him a healthy optimism and preserve him from unrealistic ventures and foolish dreams. It will enable him to perceive in all the fields, where *aggiornamento* is called for, the complexity and vastness of the task as well as the means of accomplishing it with cheerful fidelity to the Gospel and the Church. It meets the urgent need of our day: updating Christian thought, life and worship.

It is time for all Christians to become adults and to act as such. But it is the secret, the charismatic gift, of a great teacher to lead us to that constructive freedom, without which we shall remain perpetual teenagers, frightened by life or inebriated by its sudden discovery. Once again Father O'Brien has given us a superb demonstration of his ability in the most difficult of all arts: that of teaching without ever being tiresome and of inspiring and stimulating without ever being unrealistic.

AUTHOR'S INTRODUCTION

THE extent and depth of the theological renewal that has taken place in recent years is unprecedented in nearly twenty centuries of Christian history. It had its beginnings in the efforts following World War II to render the teachings and ministry of the Church more revelant to a world that had undergone such radical and profound changes. Christians in all lands had come to realize that if the world was to be spared another holocaust, that would be more destructive and horrible than ever before because of the use of nuclear weapons, religion must be made a spirit-changing catalyst in the life of humanity.

To do this, it must enter the market place, factory, office, law court and school at all levels. It must pervade the media of mass communications and profoundly influence the life of the family and the individual. This means that the emphasis must be shifted from dialectics and polemics to the positive, constructive and remedial service vital religion is capable of rendering. In short, religion must be made a pervasive and moving influence in the life of the individual and of society.

This theological renewal was further sparked by the ecumenical movement and the liturgical, vernacular and Scriptural revivals. Protestant and Catholic Biblical scholars joined forces in carrying on research in every phase of their great discipline to render the word of God intelligible to every reader. The ecumenical-minded Pope John XXIII, with his warmth and love for all men, threw the movement into high gear by convening Vatican Council II and inviting the Protestant and Orthodox Churches to send observers.

All these factors, impinging on one another, set off a chain reaction that has brought about an unprecedented ferment which has influenced every phase of theological and Biblical science. The purpose of this work is to depict the highlights of this great theological renaissance that is updating the Christian faith and practice at so many points. Since the scope of the *aggiornamento* is too extensive to be covered in a single volume, we have selected those phases of the renewal which are of the greatest interest and significance for most readers. They show the renewal which has taken place in the internal life of the Church and in its relations with the world.

There is no rigid line of demarcation, for the developments in the interior life of the Church always have repercussions upon the outside world. Thus the ecumenical movement affects not only the members of the Church but also their relations with their separated brethren. Hence there has been no effort to group or classify the renewals on the basis of their being internal or external, since these terms are, in this case, but the concave and convex aspects of the same basic reality.

We have introduced the work with a historical chapter to show, at the outset, that the Church is a living, dynamic, generative and growing organism in which developments are natural and to be expected. If this central truth is kept in mind, it will help the reader to perceive that the current updating and renewal of Christian thought and life are not symptoms of disease or betrayal, but of health and fidelity to the divine Founder of the Christian religion.

In His infinite wisdom Christ saw fit to reveal to the infant Church only the seeds of Christian dogmas which were to unfold and develop in accordance with the ever changing environment in which the People of God on pilgrimage are to live. The wisdom of the divine plan will shine forth, we hope, on virtually every page of this study.

Since this work covers the developments in many departments of theology and Biblical science, it calls for an expertise that can be met only by drawing upon the findings of specialists in many fields. This is precisely what I have done. Hence my indebtedness is to scholars too numerous to be named individually.

I must, however, single out for special thanks: Karl Rahner, E. H. Schillebeeckx, Dom Odo Casel, Louis Bouyer, Yves Congar, Hubert Jedin, J. A. Jungmann, John H. Miller, Denis O'Callaghan, A. M. Roguet, Jean Danielou, Henri de Lubac, Karl Adam, Gregory Baum, Charles Davis, John Courtney Murray and particularly my friend of many years, Godfrey Diekmann, the leader of the liturgical movement in the U.S. Their scholarly works were of special help to me in covering the many developments treated in this volume.

In addition to helping me by their works, my colleagues, John H. Miller and Louis Bouyer—fortunately for me a visiting professor here while I was writing this book—read considerable portions of the manuscript and favored me with criticisms and suggestions. I am also indebted to my confrere, Charles H. Sheedy, for suggestions regarding the organization of the topics treated, to Cardinal Cushing for his Preface, and to Father Bouyer for his Foreword. I would like to believe that the volume, embodying the ripe thought of so many of our leading scholars, will be of significance and help to members of all faiths and will, with God's grace, give further impetus to the great movement for Christian unity—the hope, prayer and dream of Christians in all lands.

John A. O'Brien

ACKNOWLEDGEMENTS

WE wish to thank the following publishers for permission to quote briefly from the following publications.

Louis Bouyer, "The Sacramental System," in *Sacraments,* edited by Denis O'Callaghan, Sheed and Ward, New York, 1964.

Catholic Encyclopedia for School and Home, volume 6, McGraw Hill, New York, 1965.

The Constitution on the Church of Vatican Council II, with a Commentary by Gregory Baum, O.S.A., The Paulist Press, Glen Rock, N.J., 1965.

Godfrey Diekmann, O.S.B., *Come, Let Us Worship,* Helicon, Baltimore, 1961.

Godfrey Diekmann, O.S.B., "Two Approaches to Understanding the Sacraments," in *Education and the Liturgy: Proceedings of the 18th North American Liturgical Week,* The Liturgical Conference, Elsberry, Mo., 1958.

Paul Palmer, S.J., "Salvation—a Sacramental Encounter," in *Current Trends in Theology,* edited by D. J. Wolf and J. V. Schall, Doubleday, New York, 1965.

Karl Rahner, S.J., and Herbert Vorgrimler, S.J., *Theological Dictionary,* Herder and Herder, New York, 1965.

Edward Schillebeeckx, *Christ the Sacrament of the Encounter with God,* Sheed and Ward, New York, 1963.

Anscar Vonier, O.S.B., *A Key to the Doctrine of the Eucharist,* Newman Press, Westminster, 1956.

CATCHING UP WITH THE CHURCH

I.

THE CHURCH
DEVELOPING THROUGH THE AGES

THIS book treats of the renewal, reform, updating and adjustments which are taking place in the internal and external life of the Church today. For the most part, they are the results of the ecumenical movement and particularly of the measures enacted by the Second Vatican Council to achieve the *aggiornamento* or updating which was the principal objective for which Pope John XXIII convoked the Council. The conditions of life had undergone such profound and far-reaching changes since the previous ecumenical council almost a century ago, that the pontiff deemed it necessary to update the life and ministry of the Church to meet more effectively the needs of a radically changed world—one which our grandfathers would scarcely recognize.

Every change, whether in thought or action, involves effort, struggle and not infrequently discomfiture and even pain. They normally occasion some temporary tension, confusion and dismay. This is true particularly if the habits of thought and action have been crystallized for many generations. Hence it is not to be wondered at that many Catholics are somewhat disconcerted and a bit bewildered by the changes which have been occasioned by Vatican Council II.

Much of this confusion stems from the failure to realize that the Church is a living organism which, like all forms of life, reacts toward changes in its environment by making appropriate adjustments. An organism which fails so to adjust is in danger of petrification, fossilization and ultimate extermination: three enemies more deadly than the horsemen of the Apocalypse.

A second source of this dismay is the failure to understand that the deposit of faith, the doctrines of divine revelation, given to the Church by Christ, were in their germinal form. Like the seeds of mighty sequoias, they were to develop through the centuries into carefully formulated statements of dogmas integrated into a creed. One may see no resemblance between the tiny acorn and the giant oak, but the whole tree is present there in germinal form, and needs but time, nourishment and sunshine to unfold its hidden potentialities. So it is with the doctrines of the Church.

"The Gospel of Christ," writes Karl Adam, "would have been no living gospel, and the seed which He scattered no living seed, if it had remained ever the tiny seed of A.D. 33, and had not struck root, and had not assimilated foreign matter, and had not by the help of this foreign matter grown up into a tree, so that the birds of the air dwell in its branches."

The Development of Doctrine

This is the central thesis which Cardinal Newman develops in his *Essay on the Development of Christian Doctrine.* In his exhaustive study of the Church in the first four centuries he found in seminal or embryonic form all the great dogmas of the Catholic Church in England in his day. This was the discovery which perhaps more than any other drew the great scholar of Oxford University into the historic Mother Church of Christendom.

This too is the magnet which brought into the fold of Christ many other great students of history. This is what attracted Ross J. S. Hoffman, professor of history at Fordham University. "I had come," he said, "to see clearly what, it seems to me, so many persons fail to grasp, namely that *Catholicism is an organic whole springing from the germinal seeds of the Incarnation.*" To him, this discovery was the keystone to the whole arch of Christianity.

Christ did not give to the Apostles an encyclopedia covering every detail of doctrine. Neither did He give them a complete blueprint of the organization of His Church nor of the detailed manner in which it was to carry on its operations in every country and in every age. Christ gave the Apostles the seed of doctrines which, under the vivifying power of the Holy Spirit, were to unfold and grow into full-orbed dogmas.

This is what Jesus meant when He said to His disciples: "Many things yet I have to say to you, but you cannot bear them now. But when he, the Spirit of truth, has come, he will teach you all truth" (Jn. 16:12–13). Throughout nineteen centuries the Spirit of truth has been breathing into the Church His spirit and stimulating the seeds of truth to grow and develop. The truths of the Gospel undergo not an evolution, in the sense of emerging from one species into another, but a development.

The process is, as St. Vincent of Lérins pointed out in the fifth century, more like the growth and development that occurs in a human being. Though the infant grows in size, in the maturity of his thought and in the deeper comprehension of truth, his personal identity remains. So it is with the development of the germinal doctrines of the Church. What was implicit in the Scriptural teaching gradually over the centuries became explicit.

Readers may be startled and even a bit shocked when we point out that St. Peter, chief of the Apostles and the first pope, could not have passed the religion examination of a fourth grade class today. He could not have answered such simple questions as: "How many sacraments are there?" "How many persons are there in God?" The theology of the sacraments was not as yet worked out nor their number determined. Neither was the doctrine of the persons in God, which we call the Most Holy Trinity. Centuries were required to develop the answers to these and scores of other questions, which the average Christian child knows today.

The Church: A Developing Organism

Hence a brief sketch of the history of the Church as a dynamic, living, growing and developing organism will help the reader both to understand and appreciate the striking developments which are occurring in the internal and external life of the Church today. History holds the key, therefore, to the proper understanding of many phenomena puzzling the Christian of our day.

Born of the Virgin Mary in Bethlehem of Judea about 7 B.C., Jesus spent nearly all of His private life in Nazareth. At the beginning of His public ministry He selected twelve Apostles and began the preaching of the Kingdom of God. He confirmed His teaching with miracles, fulfilled the prophecies of the Old Testament concerning the expected Messiah and died on Calvary's Cross.

Christ arose from the dead, appeared over a period of forty days to the Apostles and instructed them further concerning His teachings. He promised that the Father would send upon them the Holy Spirit who would recall to their minds all the truths He had revealed to them. Upon a mountain in Galilee Jesus met with His Apostles for the last time and there commissioned them to teach all nations in His name.

"All power," said Jesus, "in heaven and on earth has been given to me. Go, therefore, and make disciples of all nations, baptizing them in the name of the Father, and of the Son, and of the Holy Spirit, teaching them to observe all that I have commanded you; and behold, I am with you all days, even to the consummation of the world" (Mt. 28:18–20). Here we have the formal establishment of the Church as a living organism, the Mystical Body, of which Christ is the Head and we are the members.

Upon the morning of Pentecost when the Apostles were assembled in the Cenacle, the Holy Spirit in the form of parted tongues of fire descended upon each of them. Endowed with the gift of tongues, the Apostles began that very day to preach the Gospel to multitudes in Jerusalem and baptized 3,000 souls. Hence Pentecost is the birthday of the Church, the day on which she launched her world-wide mission. A few days later the number of believers reached the 5,000 mark.

Here is the visible evidence of the miraculous working of the Holy Spirit within the Church. Scarcely less spectacular than the miracle of the resurrection is the miracle of the Church's phenomenal growth. From a little group of 120 members on Pentecost morning, the People of God have grown into the largest religious body in the world.

Though the Gospel was first preached to the Chosen People of Israel, the Church's greatest growth was among the Gentiles. Her first major problem was to free herself from the swaddling clothes of her Jewish birth in order to receive Gentiles without imposing upon them circumcision and the other requirements of Judaism.

Paul, once a persecutor of Christians, was miraculously converted while on the road to Damascus, and soon became the leader in the struggle to free the infant Church from the shackles of the Judaic Law. It is one of the great tragedies and ironies of history that the people of the Old Covenant refused to accept Jesus as the long promised Messiah. Consequently the Church's greatest growth has ever since been among the Gentiles.

Rome was then the mightiest empire of the ancient world, extending from the Atlantic on the west to the Euphrates on the east. From the banks of the Danube and the Rhine to the cataracts of the Nile, her will was supreme. From Palestine came Christian missionaries to proclaim the good tidings of Christ. Despite ten persecutions launched against it, the Christian faith triumphed, and the blood of martyrs became the seed of Christians.

With such remarkable speed was the spiritual conquest of the Roman empire accomplished that Tertullian, a convert in the second century, was able to address to the Roman emperor the memorable words: "We are but of yesterday, and we fill all that is yours: your cities, islands, military posts, boroughs, council chambers, camps, palace, senate and forum. Your temples alone we leave you." This triumph over imperial Rome was all the more remarkable since it was accomplished without force of arms, political power, wealth or great human learning. The gap between the means used and the effect achieved demands the intervention of a divine power and reveals the supernatural character of the Christian religion.

A Miracle of the Moral Order

The victory was a miracle of the moral order and illustrates the truth of St. Paul's memorable words: "The foolish things of the world hath God chosen that he might confound the wise; and the weak things of the world hath God chosen that he might confound the strong. And the base things of the world, and the things that are contemptible hath God chosen, and the things that are not, that he might bring to nought things that are, that no flesh should glory in his sight" (1 Cor. 1:27-29).

The faith had been planted in Rome by the Apostles Peter and Paul and both died there as martyrs, according to tradition, on the same day. The Eternal City thus became the seed of the successors of Peter and the historic center of the Christian Church. That the vicar of Christ on earth should be the bishop of imperial Rome, the Mistress of the World, seems to be not only the logic of history but also the design of divine Providence. The prestige of fame of the greatest city of the ancient world thus fell upon the papacy, the highest office of the Church, thus enormously enhancing Christendom's primatial see.

Following the military conquest of Rome by Constantine in 312, a joint decision of Constantine and his Eastern colleague, Licinius—the Edict of Milan (313)—terminated the persecution throughout the empire, and granted all men the right to worship "whatever he pleases." It also compensated the Church for all the losses of the last ten years. While such toleration came to the Christians as relief, it raised the old question of Christ and Caesar in a new and dangerous form and opened the door to a legion of heresies.

Chief of these was Arianism which denied the divinity of Christ. At the emperor's orders the Council of Nicea—the first ecumenical council—was held in 325; the heresy was condemned and Arius was banished. For the first time the State had intervened not merely to summon a council but also to punish a heretic. The intervention opened Pandora's box of many ills, setting a precedent for the numerous interventions of the State in the internal affairs of the Church in the centuries to come.

In reacting to the Arian heresy, the Church, like every living organism, sought to fortify herself against that danger by formulating the Nicene creed which became integrated into the Mass and ever since has remained a part of the Church's liturgy. It is a capital instance of how heresies have provoked the Church to take remedial action to affirm more explicitly and often in stronger terms the doctrines which were either questioned or denied.

When a person cuts his finger, the body sends thousands of leucocytes, like so many firemen hurrying to a fire, to stop the flow of blood. In somewhat similar manner the living organism of the Body of Christ reacts to heal itself when wounded by heresy.

The heresy of Nestorianism was set forth by Nestorius (381–435), patriarch of Constantinople. He maintained that there were two distinct persons in Christ: the human person and the divine person. This implies that the union between the divine and the human element was merely a moral one and hence that the Word dwelt in

Jesus like a man in a house. Thus Christ was not born in His human nature from the Virgin, and hence Mary cannot properly be called the Mother of God but only the Mother of the man Christ. This means that in the Eucharist we do not receive our Lord but only the man Jesus.

To remove this danger to the faith, the third ecumenical council, that of Ephesus, was held in 431. The heresy was condemned, its author was deposed, and the divine maternity of the Virgin, along with the right to the title "Mother of God," was solemnly affirmed. While Mary is the mother of the human nature of Jesus, since this subsists in Him as in a unique person, namely, the Second Person of the Blessed Trinity, she can be properly called the Mother of God. This decision gave a mighty impetus to that special devotion to the Blessed Virgin which we find in both the Eastern and the Western Church.

The Beginning of Monasticism

Thus if space permitted, it could be shown that virtually every ecumenical council was called to condemn some heresy and thereby fortify and formulate more explicitly the doctrine attacked. What was unique about Vatican Council II was that it was summoned not to condemn any heresy but to deepen and renew the Church's own life, to update her doctrines and ministry, and to increase the relevance of both to the clamorous needs of a world wrestling with the complex and bewildering problems of multi-megaton nuclear bombs and a population soaring at a rate unprecedented in human history.

From the earliest days of Christianity certain individuals of both sexes consecrated themselves to God through a vow of chastity and withdrew from the world to devote themselves to a life of prayer, meditation and mortification. This was the beginning of monasticism. The anchorites differed from the hermits in living near one another in communities, in which each monk, however, had his separate hut and lived apart from his fellows. As time went on, Church authorities began to set strict regulations for their way of life and for some devotional exercises in common.

The next stage in the development was the establishment of communities with a common way of life under the direction of a superior. This was the beginning of monasticism in the strict sense, and the first monastery was that established by St. Pachomius at Tabennisi in Upper Egypt about 320. The rule of St. Basil of Caesaria (330–379) has remained the standard norm for monasticism in the East to this day.

From Egypt monasticism spread to the West, where its principal promoters were St. Ambrose, St. Jerome, St. Martin of Tours, St. Cassian and St. Augustine. There too it was characterized largely by its emphasis on contemplation. This was changed by the reform of St. Benedict (480–550), who balanced the contemplative life with an active one, stressing the importance of work as well as of prayer. Withdrawing from Rome, he went to live a life of meditation and mortification at Subiaco. Here a community of other monks grew up around him. These he formed into twelve monasteries, each with an abbot appointed by himself.

When jealousies broke out, he moved to Monte Cassino, where he laid the foundations of the great Benedictine monastery on a hill, the site of a former pagan temple. The famous "Rule" which he drew up requires that prayer and meditation be balanced with intellectual and manual labor. The latter means especially the cultivation of the fields and tending of the flocks needed for the support of the monks. Each monastery or abbey was separate and directed by an abbot, under whom the members lived in fraternal equality.

The order spread rapidly throughout the West, and the monasteries served as places of refuge not only for Christians but also for the intellectual treasures of the past. Thus the classics of pagan civilization were handed on to posterity. The medieval world derived immense educational, social, economic, political and spiritual benefits from the life and work of the Benedictines.

They also made an important contribution to the fusion of the various races and the advancement of a new social order by their emphasis upon fraternity and devotion to the Christian ideal of life, and thus laid the foundations of modern civilization. In their monasteries the liturgy was carried out with great reverence and dignity and, under their fostering care, reached new heights of beauty and devotion.

The Church and Society

Throughout the Middle Ages the Church entered fully into the life of the people and made their concerns her own. She established schools and universities, orphan asylums, homes for the aged, hospitals, leprosaria, institutions for the blind, and establishments to minister to every human need. Her institutions of mercy and charity dotted the medieval landscape and showed her eager determination to put into daily practice Christ's law of universal love.

Because of her concern for all the needs of men, the Church became involved in every phase of their life. Seeking to preserve peace and concord between Christian rulers and to protect the rights of their subjects, the popes became involved in politics with all the dangers such involvements inevitably entail. But politics is not immune from the law of Christ. Rulers not less than subjects need to be reminded that they all owe obedience to the divine Author of the moral law, who alone can provide effective sanctions for its observance.

Entering deeply into the life of the Greco-Roman empire, the Church assimilated both the culture of Greece and Rome. Speaking first the Aramaic language of Palestine, the Church found it necessary to adopt, as her official language, Greek, the prevalent language of the empire. After a few centuries when Latin became the common tongue of the area surrounding Rome, the Church adopted it in her liturgy. The criterion for her selection was that of maximum intelligibility and therefore of greatest service to her children.

The thirteenth century saw the establishment of two great religious orders: the Order of Friars Minor founded by St. Francis of Assisi in Italy, and the Order of Friars Preachers founded by St. Dominic in France. The Franciscans devoted themselves chiefly to preaching, missionary, educational and charitable work, the latter principally to preaching, literary and scholarly pursuits. Growing with great rapidity, these two orders deepened the spiritual life of the Church and helped her combat worldliness, indifference and heresy. Both orders established their own special schools and colleges and furnished the greatest Doctors of the day.

St. Thomas: Angelic Doctor

The chief spokesman of the Dominican order, St. Thomas Aquinas (1225–1274), the Angelic Doctor, studied at Naples, Paris and Cologne, where his teacher, St. Albertus Magnus, recognized his extraordinary genius. In his famous philosophical and theological works he gave expression to a form of Scholasticism later known as "Thomism." Taking over the best of Aristotle's thought, he developed it and showed it to be in harmony with Christian philosophy.

He stressed the distinction between philosophy and theology and insisted upon the rights of philosophy as an independent and autonomous science. Reason and faith, he maintained, are distinct. In its own domain reason is supreme. As that domain is limited, however, there are some truths which reason cannot discover, and other truths, known through divine revelation, which reason cannot demonstrate to be true.

His great synthesis of theology, *Summa Theologica,* is characterized by clarity of thought and inexorable logic; it has been widely acclaimed by scholars of all faiths as a masterpiece unsurpassed in all history. His writings, like those of all original thinkers, seemed so revolutionary to his contemporaries that they aroused intense opposition. On several occasions they were condemned by the theologians of Paris as well as by prelates and superiors of his own order. Ranking as probably the greatest of the Scholastics, St. Thomas was proclaimed "Patron of the Schools" by Pope Leo XIII.

The principal spokesman of the Franciscans was the "Seraphic Doctor," St. Bonaventure (1221–1274). He studied at Paris under the great scholar, Alexander of Hales. His writings are characterized by mysticism, profound learning and logic, and entitle him to an important place among the great Scholastics. As general of his order, he acted with wisdom and foresight and, as a cardinal, he was the chief light at the Council of Lyons (1245). Among the better known of his mystical works is *The Journey of the Mind to God.*

This brief sketch of the monastic orders and of two of their intellectual leaders shows how even this comparatively withdrawn section of the Church was involved in ministering to the educational, social, material and spiritual needs of the people. The monks were not living in ivory towers, with no interest in the concerns and daily struggles of the laity. While their central preoccupation was with God and His right to our homage and love, they never forgot that second only to the love of God is love of neighbor and that love must translate itself into service.

The Development of the Liturgy

We have seen how the infant Church left the catacombs when persecutions ceased, and became involved in every phase of the life of her children. The simple liturgy of the Apostolic era, in which the Mass consisted largely in the re-enactment of the Last Supper, was expanded to include a forepart, called the Mass of the Catechumens. This consists of prayers, hymns and readings preceding the Credo, designed to further the instruction of persons preparing for baptism. Because many of the Church's doctrines were distorted by her enemies and held up to ridicule, the Church observed "the discipline of the secret," and restricted attendance at Mass proper to the initiated.

To enhance the beauty and impressiveness of the liturgy the Church gradually introduced special vestments for use in the celebration of the Mass, called in the first centuries simply the "Sacred Mysteries." Prayers and ceremonies were added to make the Mass more meaningful for the faithful. The Confiteor is said to have been introduced by Pope St. Damasus in 348, the Kyrie by Pope St. Gregory in 604, and the Gloria by Pope St. Telesphorus in 139 for use in the Midnight Mass of Christmas. In 514 it was extended by Pope Symmachus to all Sundays and feast days.

After the Gloria a prayer called the "Collect" was introduced. It was so called because the wishes or wants of the faithful were collected and expressed in it. It is said aloud, with the hands extended in a suppliant manner, as was done in the first centuries, and is so depicted in the catacombs. Pope St. Alexander, martyred in 119, decreed that portions of Holy Scripture, chiefly the Epistles and Gospels, should be read at Mass. Hence after the Collect we have today the reading of a passage of Holy Writ, usually taken from one of the Epistles.

This is followed by the reading of a selection from one of the Gospels. St. Justin Martyr (167) tells us it was the practice after the Gospel to preach a homily which consisted largely of an explanation of the Scriptures just read, and of their application to the lives of the faithful. At this point the catechumens were dismissed.

If space permitted, the data on the introduction of the other prayers of the Mass could be presented in similar detail. Enough has been given to enable the reader to see that neither our Lord nor the Apostles prescribed all the prayers or ceremonies of the Mass. These are the result of the Church's efforts over the centuries to enhance the beauty, meaning and fruitfulness of the Holy Sacrifice for the faithful in attendance. It brings out the important truth that lies at the very heart of this book and is implicit in every chapter: the Church is a living, growing, dynamic, developing organism who adapts herself to her changing environment and to the ever varying needs of the People of God. Hence it is not too much to say that if the Apostle Peter had witnessed the elaborate ceremonies of the Solemn Pontifical High Mass which opened Vatican Council II, he would not have known what was going on. So greatly has the modern Mass developed from the simple action of Christ in consecrating the bread and wine at the Last Supper and then in giving the consecrated elements to the Apostles. The acorn has grown into a mighty oak.

The Protestant Reformation

We come now to the great religious upheaval of the sixteenth century, called the Reformation. It shook Christendom to its very foundations and brought about cleavages which fragmentized the body of Christ as never before in its long history. There were many conditions and factors which set the stage for that explosion. One of these was the growth of nationalism in the fourteenth and fifteenth centuries. The passions of nationalism began to assert themselves with the emergence of the modern concept of the State. Collisions between the officials of the Church and those of the State became the order of the day.

Besides the disruptive force of growing nationalism, the Babylonian Captivity (1307–1377) and the Western Schism (1378–1417) enormously weakened papal prestige. The Babylonian Captivity covers the seventy-year period during which popes exercised their authority from Avignon, France. They thus severed the awesome tradition which had for so many centuries associated the see of Peter with the Eternal City and made it stand out as the center of worldwide unity.

The Western Schism covers the interval of nearly forty years during which there were different claimants for the papacy. This was a scandal to all Christendom and blurred both the authority of the Church and the sense of its unity. In addition to these internal factors, there were widespread worldliness and a decline in morals among the laity, clergy and members of the papal curia. Through the use of the royal *placet* and the right of investiture, feudal lords and kings had placed worldly courtiers in bishoprics and other high places, inflicting immeasurable harm upon the spiritual life of the Church.

Then, too, there were abuses in regard to the practice of indulgences, with a wholly disproportionate emphasis upon donations. The worldly spirit introduced by the Renaissance and humanism further weakened the moral and religious life of both clergy and laity. For more than a century holy men and women within the Church had prayed and worked for a reform of the Church in its root and branches.

This was the inflammable material which Martin Luther kindled into flames in 1517 when he nailed his ninety-five theses to the doors of the church in Wittenberg. His revolt against Church authority was supported by many of the princes and, as the movement spread throughout much of Europe, vast numbers were torn from the ancient faith. The reformers proceeded to attack the authority of the Church and some of its doctrines, especially those concerning indulgences, justification, vows, the Mass and the sacraments.

The Council of Trent (1545–1563) was summoned to bring about needed reforms within the Church and to meet the attacks on Catholic doctrine. In sessions held interruptedly during the reigns of Paul III, Julius III and Pius IV over an eighteen-year period, the Council launched the Counter-Reformation and issued a great number of decrees. They covered the rule of faith, the nature of justification, grace, faith, original sin and its effects, the seven sacraments, the sacrificial nature of the Mass, the veneration of saints, use of sacred images, belief in purgatory, the doctrine of indulgences and the jurisdiction of the whole Church. The Council instituted many reforms for the renewal of the liturgy and of discipline, the promotion of religious instruction and the establishment of seminaries for the education of the clergy.

A Twofold Truth

This brief sketch of the Reformation and the Counter-Reformation brings out vividly the twofold truth that the Church has a large human element which is forever subject to reform and a divine element, which will always implement the promise of Christ to Peter: "Thou art Peter, and upon this rock I will build my Church, and the gates of hell shall not prevail against it" (Mt. 16:18). This brief sketch will enable the reader, we hope, to understand more clearly the turbulent, controversial atmosphere in which the Council Fathers discussed the articles under attack and will explain certain emphases which are now being modified, especially in the treatment of the sacraments.

The violent assault from so many quarters caused the Church to retreat into a fortress, lower the drawbridge, and have as little communication as possible with the enemy. This is the "siege" mentality that has continued for four centuries and which Vatican Council II and the whole ecumenical movement are seeking to modify.

Second only to the Council of Trent in pushing the Counter-Reformation was the Society of Jesus. Founded by St. Ignatius of Loyola, and approved by a papal bull in 1540, this company was organized along military lines and accomplished wonders in halting the progress of heresy and in regaining great sections for the historic Christian faith. Within an incredibly short time these new soldiers of Christ, fighting with the weapons of knowledge and holiness of life, largely decided the issue in France, helped mightily in saving what was saved in the Netherlands, and were in many ways responsible for snatching Poland from the peril into which it appeared likely to fall.

Another revolution which shocked the Church and made her suspicious of so-called Liberalist movements was the French Revolution, beginning in 1789. It started by confiscating the property of the Church and then imposing upon it the Civil Constitution of the Clergy, removing them from the jurisdiction of ecclesiastical authority. The priests who opposed the Constitution were tracked down, imprisoned, exiled or sent to the guillotine. In the climax of their attack upon the Church, the revolutionaries set up in place of Catholicism the cult of reason, and in 1793 enthroned an actress as the Goddess of Reason on the high altar of the Cathedral of Notre Dame in Paris.

With the memory of the bloody excesses of the French Revolution in their minds, the popes of the nineteenth-century restoration (1800–1878) had a definite bias against Liberalism in all its forms. While all of them were good men, none of them really understood the new world, which the Revolution had produced or how to convert it. The climax of those five popes, wedded to absolutism, opposed to change and scornful of popular liberty and democracy, was the last one, Pius IX (1846–1878). His *Syllabus of Errors,* issued in 1864, has been for years the despair of Catholic apologists in all democratic countries.

His reign of 32 years, the longest in the annals of the papacy, was in a political sense a succession of political disasters. Confronted with the political and military turmoil of Italy, Pius IX turned his back upon the world and, upon the confiscation of the papal states by Garibaldi in 1860, became the "prisoner of the Vatican." As an additional measure of protest, Catholics were forbidden to vote in the elections. Thus once again the drawbridge was raised and the Vatican was isolated from the contemporary world.

Lowering the Drawbridge

By a stroke of good fortune or, rather, an act of divine Providence, Pius IX was succeeded by an altogether different type of man, Leo XIII. With his election in 1878, a new era began in the Church. The drawbridge was lowered and the scholarly, far-visioned pontiff labored tirelessly for 25 years to bring the Church into contact with all the problems of men in a changing world. He knew that the days of the *ancien régime* were over, and that democracy was becoming the order of the day. Among his many great encyclicals, his *The Condition of the Working Classes* is best known and is considered epoch-making. The great pope breathed new life and energy into every phase of the Church's ministry in all lands.

His successors, Popes St. Pius X, Benedict XV, Pius XI and Pius XII, continued his work. With the election of John XXIII, however, a new era was begun: the Johannine era of the *aggiornamento*. It called for the deepening and internal renewal of the Church's spiritual life, the ecumenical movement and the dialogue with the world and all mankind. Vatican Council II launched these movements on a scale unprecedented in history. The convening of that Council and the spirit he breathed into it are his enduring monuments.

The great program he launched has been continued by his able successor, Paul VI, who made the goals of his predecessor his own. Thus a new history for the Church, Christendom and all mankind is in the making. The following chapters will present some of the highlights of that history, particularly the measures enacted by the Council to bring about a needed renewal in the Church's interior life and in her ministry to the changed world in which we live.

II.

THE VERNACULAR RENEWAL

One of the changes in the liturgy which has brought perhaps the greatest joy to Catholics, clergy as well as laity, is the greater use of the vernacular in the Mass and in the sacraments. This has been the hope, prayer and dream of the faithful for centuries. What is more natural than the desire to understand the readings, chants and prayers of the Holy Sacrifice which one attends and of the sacraments which one receives?

That wish has been fulfilled in part by the concessions already embodied in the *Constitution on the Sacred Liturgy*. There is the possibility that it may be fulfilled in its entirety by the authority granted to territorial conferences of bishops further to extend the use of the vernacular, subject only to the approval of the Holy See. This would seem to harmonize perfectly with the desire of the Council, as expressed in the constitution (# 34), that the liturgy should "be accommodated to the capacity of the faithful."

That the greater use of the vernacular in the Mass, sacraments and sacramentals is not an innovation but a renewal and a return to the practice of the Church in the Apostolic era can best be seen from a brief historical sketch of the use of languages in the liturgy. In Palestine at the time of Our Lord the language used by the Jews was Aramaic. Indeed, the Judeo-Christian communities throughout all Palestine used Aramaic until their dispersion around the year 70. With the spread of Christianity through the countries along the Mediterranean, Greek, the dominant language of those regions, came to be used in the liturgy. It was used for the sole and simple reason that it was most widely understood by the people. For two centuries it remained the principal liturgical language of the Church.

As missionaries went farther from the Mediterranean littoral and its large cities into the towns and rural areas, Armenian, Coptic and Syrian gradually came into use in the regions where they were the national languages. Toward the end of the fourth century Greek had gradually faded from common use in Rome and was replaced by the more widely used Latin. For this reason alone Latin became the tongue commonly used in the Western Church's liturgy. This change took place during the pontificate of Pope St. Damasus who reigned from 366 to 384.

History does not record whether or not there were diehards who protested against the innovation, saying: "Greek alone is a sacred language, in which we must worship God and pray to Him, even if we don't understand a word we're saying. What was good enough for our forefathers for the last 200 years should be good enough for us and our descendants. To use this new Latin tongue, worldly and pagan as it is, would be to destroy the unity of the Church and open the door to many heresies. It is a language incapable of expressing Catholic doctrine with accuracy, or prayer and homage with dignity and majesty."

From the fifth century on came the gradual emergence of the Romance languages—debased Latin dialects. Though spoken increasingly by the people in the West, they had not yet achieved acceptable literary form and none of them was, for many years, a written language. This confronted the Church with a real dilemma. None of the emerging Romance languages was as yet sufficiently stable or developed to be suitable for the liturgy; on the other hand, Latin was fading out of colloquial use and consequently was being understood less and less.

A Costly Toll

Latin was, however, retained in the liturgy, but its retention exacted a costly toll. With the people no longer able to follow the sense of the words, the Canon of the Mass, sung aloud for centuries, came to be recited by the celebrant at first in a low voice and later in utter silence. With the Mass becoming increasingly clericalized and decreasingly understood by the faithful, attendance greatly declined and the reception of Holy Communion fell to a low ebb. "A barrier had been erected between altar and nave," Godfrey Diekmann observes, "that was not effectually removed until the twentieth century, a barrier of which the roodscreen in later Gothic churches was only a logical external expression."

By the early Middle Ages vast numbers of the faithful did not receive the Holy Eucharist even once a year. Even devout laymen, such as St. Thomas More of England and St. Louis IX of France, approached the holy Table but three or four times a year. In the thirteenth century the chalice was withdrawn from the faithful when they were communicating.

The people having no active role at Mass and not really understanding what the priest was doing or saying at the altar, the Mass came to be regarded more as a theophany, a spectacular apparition of God upon the altar than as a communal sacrifice and a Paschal meal. Hence there arose the cult of "seeing God" at the elevation of the Host in the Mass—a weak substitute for receiving the holy Eucharist.

The missionaries sent by Rome to evangelize the nations in the West brought with them the Latin rite with Latin as the liturgical language. In this way Latin became the language used largely by the Church in the West. An exception to this occurred in the ninth century when the brothers Sts. Cyril and Methodius evangelized the Slavic peoples.

With might and main they struggled for the use of the Slavic languages in the liturgy, and secured authorization from Pope Nicholas I. This was displeasing to both the German princes and bishops. The princes had designs on the political autonomy of the Moravians and the bishops on their ecclesiastical independence. After the death of Cyril, Methodius was seized and imprisoned for two years. As Nicholas I had died, he appealed to John VIII, then reigning (872–882). Despite the formidable opposition of the German princes and bishops, the pope sustained Methodius and renewed the permission to use the native languages.

Pope John pointed out that holy Scripture called on all nations to praise God. Furthermore, he declared, the Apostles, filled with the Holy Spirit, proclaimed the glad tidings in all languages. Hence the celebration of Mass in the Slavic tongues was in no way con-

trary to the faith, as God had created all languages for His praise
and glory.

Sts. Cyril and Methodius might well be regarded as the advocates
and patrons of the vernacular in the liturgy. They were, however,
centuries ahead of their time. With the exception of the Slavic regions which they evangelized, Latin prevailed as the liturgical language in the West. It was never received, however, into the liturgy
of the East, where today Catholics and the Orthodox Churches
celebrate Mass in eleven languages: Greek, Armenian, Coptic, Syr-
iac, Ethiopic, Old Slavonian, Georgian, Arabic, Malayalam, Hun-
garian and Rumanian.

New Developments

By the later Middle Ages the Romance languages—French, Span-
ish, Italian, Portuguese and Catalan—had achieved sufficient maturity, suppleness and stability to be considered literary languages. The
invention of movable types for printing made reading material
readily available to ordinary people and the Renaissance kindled
their desire to learn. Furthermore the rise of nationalism quickened
the pride of people in their national tongues.

These developments brought about a change in the attitude
toward Latin and the modern languages. It would seem as though
the time had arrived when the living languages would replace
Latin, now understood only by the small class of the elite. This
became one of the great goals of the Protestant reformers, who
brought fresh and stimulating insights into the nature of Christian
worship.

They were right in emphasizing that the Mass is an act of
corporate worship and not the solitary act of the celebrant. They
were right in pointing out that the use of a living language is of
the utmost importance in enabling the people to participate intelligently in communal worship. They were right, too, in maintain-
ing that a living tongue is an important part of the full sign of
the holy Eucharist.

Unfortunately, however, some of the reformers went too far, de-
claring that the sacraments are invalid unless celebrated in a living
tongue. Thus John Calvin (1509-1564) asserted that "the sacraments

take their value from the word when it is understood; without this, they are not worthy of the name sacrament." In their emphasis upon the importance of hearing and understanding the word of God, the reformers declared that sanctification is brought about by faith which is kindled by the preaching of the Gospel. Thus the pulpit replaced the altar and the Mass became either unimportant or an "abomination." The sacraments were downgraded as of little or no value.

Because the vernacular movement was associated almost exclusively with the Protestant reformers, the Council of Trent was reluctant to make startling concessions for fear that they would appear as approving the doctrines of the reformers. With Calvin's reasons for insisting upon the vernacular in their minds, the Council Fathers condemned the assertion that "Mass must be celebrated only in the vernacular." They were careful, however, not to condemn the idea of the vernacular in the Church's worship, but only the insistence that the vernacular alone must be used.

The Council further decreed that "it did not seem expedient" to replace the traditional Latin with the vernacular. They took pains to add in the same decree, however, that shepherds of souls should frequently explain the Mass and its ceremonies "during the celebration of the Mass." Thus it is evident that, in view of the upheaval and convulsion shaking almost the whole of Christendom, the Council of Trent was moderate and restrained in dealing with this subject.

Unfortunately in the succeeding centuries Catholics were inclined to make Latin a shibboleth of orthodoxy, and to regard any discussion of the advantages of a living language in the liturgy as a concession to the doctrines of the Protestant reformers. This was evidenced in France in 1661, when a movement was initiated to promote the use of the missal with vernacular translations. Strange and incredible as it seems to us today, the practice was forbidden by Pope Alexander VII under pain of excommunication.

This prohibition was renewed as late as 1857 by Pope Pius IX, and was quietly dropped only under Pope Leo XIII in 1897. Indeed in the early years of this century Catholic presses were still turning out prayerbooks which did not dare give the readers a word-for-word translation of the Canon of the Mass. Reflecting the fear and dread of the vernacular which had mounted steadily during the post-Tridentine centuries, they substituted a timid paraphrase as if they were still afraid of incurring the centuries-old excommunication.

St. Pius X Speaks

The first clear, authoritative call for a renewal of liturgical worship with the laity participating actively in it, as in the Apostolic era, came from Pope St. Pius X in 1903. After restoring Gregorian chant and urging the congregations to join in the singing of popular hymns in the vernacular, he then wrote on the need for frequent, even daily Communion. In the later years of his life he declared that a thoroughgoing reform of the liturgy of the Western Church was needed to transform the detached, silent spectators at the Mass into articulate participants.

In the encyclical *Divini Cultus* issued in 1928, Pius XI emphasized the importance of congregational participation in the sacred rites: "It is very necessary that the faithful attend the sacred services not as if they were outsiders or mute onlookers, but let them fully appreciate the beauty of the liturgy and take part in the sacred rites, alternating their voices with the priest and the choir."

Similarly in his great encyclical on the liturgy, *Mediator Dei* issued in 1947, Pius XII pointed out that in many ceremonies of the Mass "the use of the vulgar tongue can be extremely valuable for the people." During his pontificate the Roman Ritual was published in bilingual (Latin and vernacular) editions for numerous countries at the request of their bishops. Special permission for use of the vernacular with music at Mass for countries such as Germany and Czechoslovakia was granted. Even greater concessions were made for missionary countries.

During the decade preceding Vatican Council II the movement for the increased use of the vernacular in the Mass, sacraments, sacramentals and even in the Divine Office gathered great momentum and the subject was widely discussed in the Catholic press of the U.S. The Vernacular Society and its publication *Amen,* both founded by Colonel John K. Ross-Duggan, gained wider acceptance. For years this society had been given the "cold shoulder" by most bishops, who seemed to fear they would incur the displeasure of some members of the Roman Curia if they were merely to countenance its activities.

Many considered the exclusive use of Latin in the liturgy as a sort of "sacred cow" that should not even be discussed. Others contended that Latin was a hieratic language, endowed with mystical properties, which rendered it alone suitable for divine worship. Some even praised its unintelligibility on the grounds that the Eucharistic sacrifice was a mystery and hence Latin deepend the sense of mystery. The more obscured the Mass was, the more suitable it was for the laity.

Other opponents of change talked as though they thought God had designated Latin as the official language for worship and that somehow Christ and the Apostles had used it. Some argued that what was good enough for their forebears was good enough for them. Others maintained Latin should be retained because if one traveled to a foreign country he could use his Latin missal. Topping all such flimsy arguments was one that came in a letter from an elderly lady to our Bureau of Religious Research at Notre Dame. "Like most other Catholics," she wrote, "I've been attending Mass all my life without understanding what the priest was saying at the altar. Now if he were to say it in English I wouldn't feel at home. It would distract me in saying my beads. Indeed I would feel more like being in some strange church, perhaps a Protestant one." So weak and unconvincing were the arguments against any use of the living language of the worshippers, that an open-minded person would not need to read any for the pro side to be convinced the time had come for a change.

While acknowledging that Latin is the official language of the Roman Church in the liturgy as well as in administration and government, liturgists pointed out that Latin has never been the language of the whole Church and in consequence is an imperfect symbol of unity. A better symbol of unity is the content of the liturgy and not the language. The function of language is to enable a person to express his thoughts and sentiments. If the language is unintelligible, it fails in its purpose.

A sound may come forth from the lips, but it is hollow if it has no thought content. The dignity of man lies in his rational nature and this finds no outlet when the language is unintelligible. With the advance of civilization, education and culture, man is no longer satisfied with the mere parroting of words. Hence liturgists contended that the time had come for a change—the greater use of the language of the people.

Change Long Overdue

Indeed the change was long overdue. Attendance at Sunday Mass in many countries had fallen to a disturbingly low ebb: less than 10 per cent in Latin American countries, France, Italy and Spain. In Italy surveys indicate, reports Hans Küng, that "only about 15–16 per cent of those baptized consider themselves bound to go to Sunday Mass; and the picture is even more depressing when this figure is broken down: only 5–7 per cent of young people come, only 2–3 per cent of men." With all its historic monuments and stately churches, Rome, the center of Catholicism, is a depressing sight on Sunday morning with less than 3 per cent of the men entering a church.

In the U.S. where attendance has been traditionally high—the highest in any large country—the attendance has been sagging badly, especially in our large cities, as Bernard Meyer, M.M., has shown in *Lend Me Your Hands*. Here, as elsewhere, many of those who attend have come not joyously but to avoid incurring a mortal sin. They have been detached silent spectators. The cause? Undoubtedly it has been the exclusive use of Latin even in those parts of the Mass which call for the active participation of the faithful.

There has been a barrier between the sanctuary and the nave; a palpable lack of any vital link. With the exception of the few who tried to keep pace with the celebrant, the vast majority have sat in bored silence with little sense of union with what was being done at the altar. There the celebrant stood with his back turned to the congregation, reading for the most part in an inaudible tone, and in an unknown language. A greater lack of rapport could scarcely have been contrived.

Non-Catholic visitors to our Sunday services have wondered at the silence and passivity of the audience of spectators. At a loss to understand what was going on at the altar, they missed the beautiful hymns and the prayers, sung and recited in common, which give a sense of corporate worship in their own churches. "With this background in mind," says the convert Episcopalian minister, Harold R. Bronk, Jr., "consider the non-Catholic as he enters a Catholic church for Sunday Mass. As he watches his fellow worshippers—one set streaming out of church, the other in, all of them oblivious of himself and even of one another—he cannot be blamed for linking the scene to a crowded movie house.

"He is encouraged when the priest enters, preceded by the altar boys. Now, he thinks, the service will begin. He waits for the first hymn; it never comes. All of the great treasure of magnificent music and stirring words finds no place here. His feeling of strangeness, of unchurchliness, grows. It is not dispelled by what takes place at the altar. The priest stands at the banquet table of the God-man and speaks with a voice that cannot be heard in a language that cannot be understood."

Workers in the convert apostolate have long found the unintelligibility of the Sunday service to outsiders a formidable roadblock to conversion. The use of an unknown tongue and the lack of congregational singing and of audience participation leave them bewildered spectators.

The experience of Chad Walsh, the writer, is typical. Feeling the need for divine worship and seeking a Church to minister to that need, he tells of attending a Sunday Mass. He was first chagrined and then vexed at being unable to make head or tail of what was going on at the altar. Hearing no hymns or prayers he could understand, he never returned, and a potential convert was lost forever.

An important step toward remedying the situation was taken in September, 1958, when the Congregation of Rites issued an instruction calling for various degrees of participation in the Mass by the congregation and requiring each bishop to put it into effect. Starting with a few simple responses, the congregation was directed to become increasingly involved in the dialogue with the priest. The celebrant was directed to confine himself to his priestly part; neither were the acolytes or choir to substitute themselves for the congregation. Every member of the congregation was instructed to participate in the dialogue.

The Mass Calls for Participation

"By its nature," said the instruction, "the Mass calls for participation by all who are present, each in a way proper to him." It then stresses the supreme importance of *interior* participation: "The participation must above all be interior, exercised in the pious attention of the soul and in the affections of the heart, so that in this way the faithful may be united as closely as possible with the High Priest . . . and together with Him and through Him offer [His sacrifice] and offer themselves with Him."

This historic document called for a shift of emphasis and required bishops and priests to clarify the four doctrines or themes which underlie such participation and even demand it: (1) the headship and mediatorship of the divine Redeemer; (2) union with Christ by grace and the sacramental characters; (3) participation in His worship of the Father; (4) the various roles assigned men in this worship by baptism and holy orders. Thus the faithful will perceive how the liturgy enables them to enter into personal relations with God, Father, Son and Holy Spirit, with other members of the Church and with all men.

The implementation of this instruction added new cogency and urgence to the pleas for some use of the vernacular and rendered the latter inevitable. Why? Because it soon became crystal clear that the mere parroting of Latin words did not result in that interior participation upon which the instruction has particularly insisted. It did not involve the mind and heart. It was a mechanical artificial affair. Instead of experiencing interior devotion, the faithful felt irritated and bored with the effort to pronounce strange and foreign words, devoid of both intellectual and emotional content. Thus had the Sacred Congregation made some use of the living tongue inescapable.

Another mighty step toward the longed for goal was taken on the evening of March 13, 1960, when Pope John XXIII visited the Church of Our Lady of Succor in a working-class district of Rome. The church was packed with people. They sat gazing at the priests in the sanctuary who were chanting and praying in Latin, wondering what it was all about. For a half-hour this went on before a single word of Italian was spoken.

As the pope looked at the people and noted the bewildered and perplexed expressions on their faces, his heart was filled with pity. When he arose to speak, he said with fatherly compassion, "I am going to try to have more of the sacred rites in the language of the people." With the speed of lightning his words encircled the globe and brought joy to the faithful in every land.

In commenting on this timely and providential utterance of the great pontiff, the NCWC News Service said: "What he did was to promise that the Church, to show her wish to be ever closer to the people who do not know Latin, will do everything possible to make her sacred ceremonies better understood." Perhaps no other pope in so short a period so won the esteem and love not only of Catholics but of the whole world as the big-hearted, compassionate, precedent-breaking and Christlike Pope John XXIII.

Given an unexpected assist by the providential utterance of the great pontiff, the long hard struggle for some of the language of the people in the liturgy was nearing its climax. The first subject to which Vatican Council II turned its attention was the sacred liturgy, thus acknowledging its paramount importance. The use of the vernacular was discussed at great length, with spokesmen of various viewpoints mounting the rostrum.

Overwhelming Victory for Vernacular

The question was finally put to a vote on December 7, 1962. Of the 2,118 Council Fathers present, 1,922 voted in favor, 11 against, 180 in favor with reservations and 5 void. The faithful throughout the world were as surprised as they were thrilled to learn of the overwhelming majority by which the measure passed. The measure authorized territorial conferences of bishops to permit a limited use of the language of the people, subject to approval by the Holy See. Bishops were also empowered to permit their clergy to read the Divine Office in the vernacular if Latin presented difficulties to them, and they were urged to be liberal in granting such permissions.

The use of the vernacular, limited as it is, has already helped to revitalize the Mass and to increase intelligent participation. The first part of the Mass, in which the vernacular is used almost entirely, has been literally transformed. How inspiring is the sight of the whole congregation standing and singing the entrance hymn, as the celebrant, cross bearer and acolytes march down the center aisle. How joyously the people participate in the prayers and with what eager interest they listen to the Epistle and Gospel, read in their own tongue. They are now integral parts of the Mass and not, as previously, postscripts to the Latin versions read by the celebrant with his back to the congregation.

How heartwarming it is for the faithful to see one of their own at the lectern reading the Epistle for them and leading them in other prayers throughout the Mass. How pleased must Pope St. Pius X be, as he looks down from heaven upon all the members of the congregation actively participating in the Mass and singing the devotional hymns as he had pleaded for them to do.

Non-Catholic visitors no longer feel strange and ill at ease, now that some prayers and practically all the congregational hymns are in the language of the people. How delighted are the worshippers to have the priest face them as he celebrates the Holy Sacrifice and thus brings them into closer union not only with himself but also with the sacrificial Victim, Jesus Christ. Just as every previous poll had shown the overwhelming majority of both priests and parishioners to favor the introduction of the vernacular into the liturgy, so now every poll has manifested their gratification and happiness with the results.

Letters streaming into our Bureau of Religious Research from people in all parts of the country bear eloquent witness to this fact. We quote two typical ones. "I had been going to Mass," writes a middle-aged man in the east, "largely out of routine and fear of committing a mortal sin, but it meant little to me. The Mass was mumbled in Latin by a priest with his back to the congregation. There was no congregational participation either through prayer or hymns, and hence no sense of unity with the celebrant. It seemed like a carry-over from the Middle Ages.

"Now the congregation comes to life the moment the priest and acolytes start down the middle aisle. We sing together, we pray together, we worship together. I never thought I would live to see such a development. We can never sufficiently thank Pope John XXIII for calling the Council which brought about these changes."

A lady in the south writes: "I am a convert, and the thing I missed most was the use of English in the service. I like to join in the recitation of prayer and the singing of hymns. One was kept occupied all the time and knew what was going on. It was an hour I looked forward to with joy. I don't understand Latin and the mumbled prayers and actions of the priest at the altar had little meaning for me. I knew, of course, that Christ was present on the altar. But I wished that I could express my homage and love for Him more effectively than by sitting silently in the pew.

"Now it is vastly different. We pray together and sing together. My mind and heart are both involved. I hope that before long all the Mass will be said in English and that we can join in saying more of the prayers aloud. Then our participation in the Mass and our sense of unity with the celebrant will be complete."

In his widely syndicated column, "The Question Box," Monsignor J. D. Conway published the following letter as typical of the reactions of the faithful to the introduction of the vernacular in the liturgy: "I am a Grandma, about 60, and I think the changes in the Mass are the most wonderful thing that ever happened, and I remember to thank God in my prayers. It's so nice when I go to Mass and my little grandchildren sit at my side, and I hear them all say the Mass prayers with me. It gives me the feeling that everyone is getting something out of the Mass, where before the children just played with their rosaries."

What a moving tribute to the intelligibility which the use of the vernacular has brought to the Holy Sacrifice that now even children can participate in it. This, after all, was the goal which St. Pius X had in mind when he sounded his call for the changes which would render participation in the Eucharistic sacrifice possible for all. It was the goal too of all the liturgists who struggled for the changes.

A Return to the Practice of Christ

They were seeking not novelties or innovations, but a simple return to the practice of our divine Saviour and of the Apostles. At the Last Supper when Christ celebrated the first Mass, He didn't turn His back to the Apostles or speak to them in an unknown tongue. He looked into their faces and spoke to them in their own language. His gestures and actions were simple, clear and meaningful. There was no need for interpreters to explain either His words or His actions. That is the goal of the liturgists and of Vatican Council II, as expressed with crystal clarity in the *Constitution on the Sacred Liturgy*.

"To promote active participation," says the constitution, "the people should be encouraged to take part by means of acclamations, responses, psalmody, antiphons and hymns, as well as by actions, gestures and bodily attitude. The rites should be distinguished by a noble simplicity; they should be short, clear and unencumbered by any useless repetitions; they should be within the people's powers of comprehension, and normally should not require much explanation" (# 30 and # 34).

The leaders of the liturgical movement were in the vanguard of the legion of priests and laity who were striving to secure the use of the vernacular in the liturgy, especially in the Mass. They share in the general rejoicing over the action of Vatican Council II in approving at least a limited use of it. The whole Catholic world is in their debt.

In the U.S. in addition to Colonel John K. Ross-Duggan, mention should be made of Dr. Joseph Evans, former president of the Vernacular Society, and Irwin St. John Tucker whose tireless zeal and unflagging devotion were unsurpassed. Outstanding among the clergy were Gerald Ellard, S.J., H. A. Reinhold, Michael A. Mathis, C.S.C., Monsignor Robert Sherry, Godfrey Diekmann, O.S.B., C. J. McNaspy, S.J., Joseph T. Nolan, John LaFarge, S.J., and Bishop Edwin V. O'Hara. There are, of course, many other laymen and clergy who worked, struggled and prayed for the success of the vernacular movement, and all deserve our gratitude.

The discussion of this subject ends fittingly on a note of gratitude, hope and joy. So pleased were the bishops of this country over the results of the modest introduction of the vernacular into the liturgy that, while attending the fourth session of the Council, they announced plans for its more extensive use. Millions are hoping and praying that this is but another step toward the ultimate celebration of the Eucharistic sacrifice and of the sacraments in their entirety in the language of the faithful.

How inspiring it will be to hear the Canon of the Mass recited in the people's tongue and to hear the faithful join with the celebrant in that supreme act of worship, praise, atonement, gratitude and supplication. Then the faithful will be truly united not only with the celebrant but also with the sacrificial Victim in presenting to the heavenly Father the one infinitely perfect gift that can be offered on earth or in heaven.

III.

RENEWAL OF THE LITURGY

THE Christian world has heard much in recent years about the liturgy. It was one of the chief topics of discussion and debate at the first two sessions of Vatican Council II in 1962 and 1963, and reports of those talks were published in newspapers throughout the world. To most people, however, the meaning of the term "liturgy" is still somewhat vague. Hence it will be well at the outset to indicate exactly what we are talking about.

Derived from the Greek, the word "liturgy" originally meant any work of a public nature. It is now used to signify the public and official worship of the Church in the West. In the New Testament it was used to denote the worship of the Christian community and in the early Church the word was applied only to the celebration of the Eurcharist. In the Eastern rites of the Church this usage is still retained, and we find the terms "liturgy" and "Eucharist" used interchangeably.

In the Church of the Latin rite the term "liturgy" designates the entire corporate, public and official worship of the Church and thus distinguishes it from the prayers and devotions of individual members. In the Letter to the Hebrews St. Paul employs the term for the priestly work of Christ: liturgy in its distinctively Christian sense: "We have such a high priest . . . a minister [liturgist] of the Holies, and of the true tabernacle which the Lord has erected . . . and not man . . . But now he has obtained a superior ministry [liturgy], in proportion as he is the mediator of a superior covenant, enacted on the basis of superior promises" (8:1–6).

The most authoritative definition is that formulated by Pius XII in *Mediator Dei,* where he defines the liturgy as "the public worship which our Redeemer as Head of the Church renders to the

Father, as well as the worship which the community of the faithful renders to its Founder, and through Him to the heavenly Father. In short, it is the integral public worship of the Mystical Body of Jesus Christ, of Head and members."

Reflecting the dual nature of man, physical and spiritual, liturgy must be both exterior and interior. Furthermore as God endowed man with a social nature, he must acknowledge that gift by using it to join with other members of the Christian community in rendering homage to God. Hence private worship alone will not suffice.

The chief element in all worship, however, is the interior: it must come from man's mind and heart. Otherwise the posture and movements of the body and its members are meaningless. This is stressed by Pius XII in *Mediator Dei,* wherein he declares that if interior worship is lacking, "religion clearly amounts to mere formalism, without meaning and without content."

The liturgy of the Church always has a priestly quality because it is the worship of our High Priest, in which we participate by means of the power of the priesthood. In the liturgy we, the members of the Mystical Body, join with Christ its Head in offering homage to God the Father. It is His priestly participation that thus gives to our poor human homage a value that utterly transcends our power.

Christ's Priesthood—Eternal

Moreover His participation in our worship is unceasing because His priesthood is eternal. This is the point which St. Paul makes in the Letter to the Hebrews: "Because he continues forever, he has an everlasting priesthood. Therefore he is able at all times to save those who come to God through him, since he lives always to make intercession for them" (7:24-25).

By using a lever, one can move a rock which otherwise he could not budge. The longer the lever, the more powerful is the leverage. The ancient Greek physicist Archimedes is said to have exclaimed: "Give me a lever long enough and I shall move the earth!" The lever which gives to our weak human worship an infinite value and thus makes it infinitely worthy and acceptable in Christ's participation in it.

As this point is crucial and all-important, we shall illustrate it with another example. Midas, the legendary king of Phrygia, was said to have the power of turning into gold anything he touched. Greater than the legendary power of Midas, however, is the power of Christ, for every act of our worship which He touches with His divine presence is transmuted into homage more pleasing to the heavenly Father than all the gold in the world.

The public worship of the Church has a priestly quality not only because our High Priest, Jesus Christ, participates in it and offers it up with us but also because He shares His priesthood with us. Stressing this point in his first Epistle, St. Peter urges Christians to draw near to Christ, "a living stone, rejected indeed by men but chosen and honored by God. Be you yourselves as living stones built thereon into a spiritual house, a holy priesthood, to offer spiritual sacrifices acceptable to God through Jesus Christ . . . You are a chosen race, a royal priesthood, a holy nation, a people purchased by God to proclaim the great deeds of him who has called you out of darkness into his marvelous light" (2:4–9).

Such is the royal priesthood of the Christian community, which renders their communal worship so pleasing to their eternal Father and enables it to reflect the everlasting liturgy of Christ together with the angels and saints in heaven. In thus exercising their priesthood, Christians transform the worshipping community into an organ of the Mystical Body, manifesting its solidarity with its Head in His sublime and distinctive role. This St. Paul describes so aptly as that of the "one Mediator between God and men, himself man, Christ Jesus, who gave himself a ransom for all" (1 Tim. 2:5–6).

In the exercise of the liturgy, the Church enjoys a threefold share of Christ's priesthood because of the sacramental characters imprinted by baptism, confirmation and holy orders. "While Christ is the principal minister of every liturgical act," says John H. Miller, an expert on the liturgy, "He works through a variety of human agents who sacramentalize His eternal worship. The sacramental characters structure the Church, making it a hierarchical society with each member contributing his proper part toward the prolongation of redemptive Incarnation."

The Heart of the Liturgy

When Christians assemble for the Eucharistic sacrifice, the heart of the liturgy, each carries out the duties distinctive of his place in the Church. By baptism a person becomes a member of the Mystical Body, enabling him to receive other sacraments and a basic share in the priesthood of Christ. In confirmation he receives the graces to achieve spiritual adulthood and to serve as an apostle extending Christ's kingdom in the souls of others. Through holy orders a man receives the graces and power of the priesthood enabling him to preach the Gospel with authority, to pardon sinners in the name of Christ and to celebrate Mass.

He thus makes present Christ's paschal mystery for the spiritual enrichment of all the members of the Mystical Body. In this basic and central act of the liturgy, Christ continues the worship of the Father through the Christian community, the Church.

Stressing the central and climactic character of this action, Pius XII in *Mediator Dei* declared: "The mystery of the most holy Eucharist which Christ the High Priest instituted, and which He commends to be continually renewed in the Church by His ministers, is the culmination and center, as it were, of the Christian religion."

This central action of the liturgy has continued in the Church from the days of the Apostles. "And they continued steadfastly," says St. Luke, "in the teaching of the Apostles and in the communion of the breaking of the bread and in prayers" (Acts 2:42). As the seven sacraments are outward signs through which Christ brings the fruits of His redemption to the souls of the recipients, they are included in the liturgy. So too are the sacramentals and the Divine Office, by which she fulfills the injunction of St. Paul: "Teach and admonish one another by psalms, hymns and spiritual songs, singing in your hearts to God by his grace" (Col. 3:16).

The Background of Liturgical Revival

In the early centuries the bond between altar and worshippers was intimate and constantly kept alive by the dialogue between priest and people. As the Mass was read aloud in the language of the people, they needed no interpreter to explain either the prayers or the ceremonies. Their intimate participation reached its normal conclusion with virtually all receiving Holy Communion. The Mass was a collective action, with priest and people both participating in the paschal supper. If anyone asked the members of a congregation who it is that celebrates the holy Eucharist, they would have answered, "We, the people of God, celebrate the Eucharist."

At the close of the patristic era, ending with St. Gregory the Great about 600, the doctrine of the Mystical Body became obscured. In the subsequent five centuries the close bond between the celebrant and the congregation was broken. By 1100 the Mass had become almost exclusively a priestly action and service. The Mass of the Catechumens was in a language which the worshippers did not understand and the prayers of the Canon were said in utter silence.

"At the Canon," Godfrey Diekmann points out, "the priest, like Moses, climbed the sacred mountain alone and the people were left behind at the foot of the mountain, at best engaged in prayerful meditation on the events of Christ's life on the basis of an artificial, allegorical interpretation of some of the visible external rites. The inner meaning of the heart of the Mass was obscured to them."

What was the cause of such a drastic change? There were many causes. Prominent among them, research scholars are agreed, was the struggle against the Arian heresy which denied the divinity of Christ. In reacting against that heresy, so great an emphasis was placed upon His divinity that His sacred humanity was unduly minimized and obscured. This was peculiarly detrimental to the proper understanding of Christ's role in the Mass, which is that of the Redeemer who suffered and died for us. It was His humble role of a servant that He Himself emphasized at the Last Supper when He said: "I stand in the midst of you as one who serves" (Lk. 22–27).

In describing the climate of the long drawn-out anti-Arian reaction, Karl Adam observes: "Christ no longer stands by man's side as the representative and advocate of mankind; and He as the man, Christ Jesus, and the First-born of His brethren, no longer offers the sacrifice of mankind to the Triune God. He has, so to speak, crossed over, and is now on God's side, and Himself is the awful and unapproachable God."

One-Sided Emphasis

This one-sided emphasis upon Christ's divinity has continued through the years to such an extent that Christ is commonly thought of as the divine Consecrator and the Mass as a service at which God becomes present in their midst instead of the action of the faithful with and through their priests, the Church and their High Priest, the man-God, Jesus Christ. This was reflected in the attitude of the faithful, particularly in the Middle Ages, who came to Mass chiefly to "see God" at the elevation. The persistence of this attitude led inevitably to the increasing clericalization of the Mass and to the neglect of the role of the faithful.

Their non-involvement was further deepened by the retention of Latin in the liturgy of the West when it was no longer the language of the people. While it is true that the emerging Romance languages had not as yet achieved literary excellence, they were actually the only languages used and understood by the people. It was this realization that prompted Bishop Ulfilas, Apostle of the Goths in the fourth century, to translate the Scriptures into the Gothic language.

If it was considered proper to translate the Bible—a more direct and important expression of the word of God than any liturgical non-Biblical text—into the vernacular, it is difficult to understand why the prayers of the Mass were not likewise translated into the living languages of the people. The explanation of this curious enigma is to be found in the obscuring of the communal nature of the paschal meal, of the sacred humanity of Christ and consequently of the doctrine of the Mystical Body and of the Eucharist as a sacrifice and sacrament, in which all the members of Christ's body are to participate.

In his monumental work, *The Mass of the Roman Rite*, Joseph A. Jungmann, S.J., shows how the discipline of the secret (*disciplina arcani*) was employed to conceal the Church's holy things, especially the Eucharist, from the heathens. But this discipline was paralleled for more than a thousand years by another discipline which effectively hid the holy things from the members of Christ's family, the people of God, for whose spiritual nourishment they were instituted. The one-sided emphasis on the divinity of Christ with the consequent failure of the faithful to participate actively in the Mass led in both East and West to a general neglect of Holy Communion.

It led also, as we shall show in detail in the section on the sacraments, to the dimming of the concept of Christ and the Church as primordial and basic sacraments. Indeed history shows that whenever the clear perception of the glorified humanity of Christ, our elder Brother and the new head of redeemed humanity, is blurred, there can be no proper understanding of the Church as the Mystical Body and the perpetuation of Christ's saving humanity through space and time. Here too is the explanation of the relegation, for so many centuries, of Christ's resurrection to a secondary and largely apologetic role in the totality of our redemption.

The Awesome Mystery of the Incarnation

Through the centuries there has been a tendency for Christians to shy away from the awesome, baffling and even frightening mystery of the Incarnation: God omnipotent, omniscient, inaccessible in the far distant heavens, taking to Himself a human nature such as ours, frail and weak, so that we can say literally, *God became man,* suffered, died and rose from the dead for our redemption. In his First Letter to the Corinthians, St. Paul alludes to the mystery of the redemptive Incarnation with its climax in the crucifixion as shocking alike to Jews and Gentiles.

"We, for our part," he says, "preach a crucified Christ—to the Jews indeed a stumbling-block and to the Gentiles foolishness, but to those who are called, both Jews and Greeks, Christ the power of God and the wisdom of God. For the foolishness of God is wiser than men, and the weakness of God is stronger than men" (1:23–25). Because of the refusal of many to face up to the scandal and foolishness of the Incarnation there arose in the first century the heresy of Docetism. Its members asserted that the second person of the Trinity merely *appeared* in the form of a man, that it was no more than a fantasy created by the Logos to make Himself visible to men.

Perceiving the beginnings of this heresy, St. John the Apostle in his old age warns the faithful against it. "By this," he says, "is the spirit of God known: every spirit that confesses that Jesus Christ has come in the flesh, is of God. And every spirit that severs Jesus [considers Christ and Jesus as two distinct persons], is not of God, but is of Antichrist . . ." (1 Jn. 4:2-3).

Other Heresies

In succeeding centuries we find the same shying away from the mystery of the Incarnation erupting into other heresies. Thus in the fifth century Nestorius, Patriarch of Constantinople, and his followers asserted that in Jesus Christ a divine person and a human person were joined in perfect harmony of action but not in the unity of a single individual. They denied that the two were united in the one person of the Word of God, and hence they denied that God became man, suffered, died and rose for man.

Scarcely had the Council of Ephesus (431) condemned Nestorianism when the Monophysites began to stress the divinity of Christ to such an extent that His humanity is so badly dwarfed as virtually to disappear. Just as a drop of wine, when cast into the sea, is absorbed and disappears, so the humanity of Christ, they asserted, is absorbed into the infinite reality of His divine nature and vanishes. Thus for all practical purposes Christ has but one divine nature. Hence we cannot say that God became incarnate, suffered and died for us.

Even within the mainstream of the Catholic faith, orthodox and correct, the tendency to shrink from facing up to the full implications of the doctrine of the Incarnation has persisted through the centuries. There is, of course, no theoretical rejection, but merely a reluctance, often subconscious, to trace out the implications and put them into practice. Under the stress apparently of excessive piety the average Catholic concentrates so intensely upon the divinity of Christ as to relegate into the background His sacred humanity and the vitally important role it plays in the Mass, sacraments and worship. Ask any dozen Catholic communicants after a Sunday Mass, "Whom did you really receive?" and the majority will answer, "God."

Such then is the historical background necessary to appreciate the liturgical revival. It is that background, which could easily be amplified into many volumes, which makes that revival so necessary for the deepening of the spiritual life of the faithful and for the vitalizing of the Mass and the sacraments. Indeed it is not too much to say that the liturgical renewal was the means used by divine Providence and the Church, moved by the Holy Spirit, to restore the sacred humanity of the glorified Christ to its rightful role in the life and worship of the Church.

The Liturgical Movement

Let us now sketch briefly the origin and development of the liturgical movement, now in full fruition. Historians credit Prosper Guéranger (d. 1875), Benedictine abbot of Solesmes, France, with stimulating interest in liturgical reform with his fifteen-volume commentary, *The Liturgical Year*. In it he drew widespread attention to the superior way in which Christian piety and the spiritual life can be developed by praying *with* the Church. In Germany the writings of the nineteenth-century theologians Johann Sailer and Matthias Joseph Scheeben stressed the doctrine of the Mystical Body and pointed out its importance for a proper understanding of the liturgy.

Great impetus was given to this movement by Pope St. Pius X in his letter, "Among the Cares," issued in 1903. In it he declared that active participation in the liturgy is "the primary and indispensable source of the true Christian spirit." This became the basic principle of the liturgical movement and was further emphasized by Pius X in his decrees on frequent Communion, Gregorian chant, and the reform of the liturgical rites.

It was in Belgium that the first practical program for promoting lay participation in the liturgy was developed by Lambert Beauduin, O.S.B., under the sponsorship of Désiré Cardinal Mercier in 1918. At about this time the Benedictine monastery of Maria Laach became the intellectual center for the spread of the movement in Germany. In Klosterneuburg, near Vienna, an Augustinian, Pius Parsch, published a number of books and pamphlets which helped to promote intelligent, active participation in the liturgy by the laity.

The Liturgical Movement in the U.S.

In the United States the liturgical movement is comprised within the span of my priesthood. The person generally credited with sparking this movement there is Virgil Michel, O.S.B., of St. John's Abbey, Collegeville, Minnesota. A classmate of mine at the Catholic University in 1916, Father Michel gave the first extensive impetus to the movement by founding the Liturgical Press in 1926. Publishing works on liturgical subjects, his press brought a true understanding of the objectives of the liturgical movement to thousands of pastors. Especially influential has been its monthly review *Worship* (originally *Orate Fratres*) edited by Father Godfrey Diekmann, the outstanding leader of the movement for many years. Some of the others sharing in the leadership are Bishop Edwin V. O'Hara, Gerald Ellard, S.J., H. A. Reinhold, Martin Hellriegel and my late confrere, Michael A. Mathis, C.S.S.

In the early years liturgists labored under a cloud of suspicion and misunderstanding. Many considered them cranks, interested chiefly in ecclesiastical millinery, in rubrics and items external and peripheral to the worship of the Church. Hence, when the first liturgical week was held in the basement of a Chicago church in 1940, only a couple hundred people showed up. But in recent years the attendance has been so enormous, that it has become necessary to hold several liturgical conferences in different regional centers.

What has brought about the change is the unequivocal support given by recent popes. In 1943, in the midst of World War II, Pius XII set forth the theological basis for the present liturgical renewal in the encyclical *Mystici Corporis Christi*. Though it dealt directly with the nature of the Church, it indirectly set forth the liturgical movement since the latter is simply a manifestation of what the Church really is. Four years later Pius XII issued the encyclical *Mediator Dei*, the first comprehensive exposition of the doctrinal basis for the liturgical revival, which was heartily approved and strongly encouraged.

The First Major Breakthrough

In 1948 Pius XII gave further authoritative impetus to the movement by establishing the Pontifical Commission for the General Restoration of the Liturgy. This called for a thoroughgoing reform. The year 1955 will always be remembered in the history of the liturgical movement, for in that year there occurred the first major breakthrough in the liturgy of the Latin rite since the era of the Fathers. This consisted in the restored rites of Holy Thursday, Good Friday and Holy Saturday.

Before 1955 Holy Week was a pathetic sight in comparison with what occurs in most parish churches today. The services took place in the morning, usually with just a few parishioners present. Sitting silently and detached, they had little, if any, understanding of what was taking place at the altar. It was a sad commentary on what should be the greatest week in the whole liturgical calendar.

In 1956 further impetus was given to the liturgical movement by the first International Congress of Pastoral Liturgy at Assisi and at Rome. There Pius XII approved its objectives and declared that the movement was an evidence of action of the Holy Spirit in drawing the faithful into active participation in the liturgical life of the Church. Instead of being a fad or an esoteric hobby for an elite few, the pope said, "It is a sign of the movement of the Holy Spirit in the Church today." Two years later, as we have seen, the Vatican issued detailed instructions for the active participation of all the faithful in the Mass throughout the entire Church in the West.

The Role of Christ's Humanity

Such participation means that the faithful must understand more clearly the role of the sacred humanity of Jesus in the Mass both as a sacrifice and as a sacramental re-enactment of the paschal meal at the Last Supper. It means too that the faithful must unite with Christ in His priestly role of worship of the Father and offer with Him, through the Holy Spirit and in union with all members of the Mystical Body, the redemptive sacrifice of Calvary. They must perceive that the sacred liturgy thus brings them into a new set of personal relations with God—Father, Son and Holy Spirit—with other members of the Church and with all mankind.

The message which the liturgical movement sought to emphasize in season and out of season was the simple one that the liturgy serves to draw the faithful closer to the heavenly Father in union with Christ. Hence it was a source of encouragement and inspiration for its leaders when Pius XII stated this simple but all-important truth in *Mediator Dei* in the following words: "It should be clear to all then that the worship rendered to God by the Church in union with her divine Head is the most efficacious means of achieving sanctity."

It was also gratifying for all engaged in the liturgical apostolate to read the comment on these words by Cardinal Montini in his 1958 Pastoral: "Hence we must welcome the liturgical renewal as the means of the religious rebirth and the form which that rebirth must take, according to the spirit and laws of Mother Church." In urging his priests and faithful to welcome the liturgical revival and to participate in it with heart and soul, Cardinal Montini listed the following reasons for such participation:

"The spiritual decadence of our times demands it. The cultural development of our people demands it. The inner vitality of holy Church demands it. The teaching authority of the Church demands it. The eternal bidding of Christ: 'Do this in memory of me,' demands it."

The Constitution on the Liturgy

The crown and climax of the whole liturgical movement was the enactment of the *Constitution on the Sacred Liturgy* by Vatican Council II. Behind this document lies an enormous amount of thought and work by a multitude of liturgical experts, theologians, Biblical scholars and clerics of all ranks. The theme was discussed by the Council Fathers at great length. There were 328 oral interventions and more than 350 written ones.

Bishops from the mission areas as well as from traditionally Catholic countries spoke on the subject with great freedom and candor at both the 1962 and 1963 sessions of the Council. The schema was rewritten many times to reflect the views and criticisms of the Fathers. From October 22 to November 13 in the first session the subject was discussed continuously.

In the second session, on November 22, 1963, the schema as a whole was approved by a vote of 2,159 to 19. On December 4, 1963, the constitution was enacted by a vote of 2,147 to 4, and promulgated on that date by Pope Paul VI together with the Council Fathers.

In promulgating it, His Holiness said: "We, by the Apostolic power given to us by Jesus Christ, *together with the venerable Fathers,* approve, decree and enact . . ." These words, spoken after the Council Fathers had expressed their will by an overwhelming vote, reveal the intention of the pope to respect the collegiality of the bishops assembled in Council. According to the terms of the promulgation, the constitution became effective on the first Sunday of Lent, February 16, 1964.

IV.

THE CONSTITUTION
ON THE LITURGY

THE first great achievement of Vatican Council II was the monumental *Constitution on the Sacred Liturgy*. If the Council accomplished nothing else, this alone would more than have justified its convocation. It has already profoundly affected the life and worship of the people of God from the top echelon to the bottom and will doubtless go down in history as the Magna Carta of divine worship. A constitution is a document which both teaches doctrine and prescribes rules of action. Because the schema on the liturgy does both, it is called a constitution.

Divided into seven chapters and 130 articles covering a wide range of topics, the constitution begins with an Introduction which sets forth the chief aims of the Council as follows: "It desires to impart an ever increasing vigor to the Christian life of the faithful; to adapt more suitably to the needs of our own times those institutions which are subject to change; to foster whatever can promote union among all who believe in Christ; to strengthen whatever can help to call the whole of mankind into the household of the Church. The Council therefore sees particularly cogent reasons for undertaking the reform and promotion of the liturgy."

As the Council's purpose was primarily pastoral, its document on the liturgy reflects that same practical concern, and seeks to quicken the spiritual life of the people of God. Instead of offering merely the comments of liturgists on the constitution, we shall endeavor to present in somewhat condensed form its more important parts, not infrequently in substantially its own phrasing to catch some of its rich Scriptural character.

The constitution points out that the liturgy, especially in the holy sacrifice of the Eucharist, is the chief means whereby the faithful can manifest in their lives the mystery of Christ and the real nature of the Church. The latter is both human and divine, present in the world and yet not at home in it. In the Church the human element is subordinated to the divine, the visible to the invisible, action to contemplation and the present world to the celestial city to which we pilgrims look forward with eager longing.

Making generous use of Scripture, the document declares that the liturgy daily builds up those who are within into a holy temple of the Lord, into a dwelling place for God in the Spirit, to the mature measure of the fullness of Christ. Moreover, it increases their ability to proclaim the glad tidings of Christ, and thus discloses the Church to outsiders as a sign lifted up among the nations, under which the scattered children of God may be brought together so that Christ's plan of one flock and one shepherd may be realized.

The constitution declares that its general principles and norms apply to the Roman rite and to all others, but that its practical norms apply only to the Roman rite except for those which, by their very nature, affect other rites as well. It then explains that the Church considers all lawfully acknowledged rites to be of equal right and dignity and wishes to preserve and foster them. Where necessary, the rites are to be revised in the light of sound tradition to meet the needs of modern times.

General Principles for Liturgical Reform

After these introductory remarks, the constitution sets forth in its first chapter the general principles for the restoration and promotion of the liturgy. In its exposition of the nature of the liturgy and its importance in the Church's life, it points out that God who "wills that all men be saved and come to the knowledge of truth" (1 Tim. 2:4), "who in diverse manners spoke in times past to the fathers by the prophets" (Heb. 1:1), when the fullness of time had come, sent His Son, the Word incarnate.

He was anointed by the Holy Spirit to preach the Gospel to the poor, to heal the contrite of heart, to be a "bodily and spiritual medicine" and the Mediator between God and man. United with the person of the Word, His sacred humanity was the instrument of our redemption. Hence in Christ "the perfect achievement of our reconciliation came forth and the fullness of divine worship was given to us."

The constitution explains that the marvelous works of God among the people of the Old Testament were merely a prelude to the work of Christ both in redeeming mankind and in giving perfect glory to God. This mission was accomplished chiefly by the paschal mystery of His blessed passion, resurrection and glorious ascension, whereby "dying, he destroyed our death and rising, he restored our life." From the side of Christ as He slept the sleep of death upon the Cross there came forth "the wondrous sacrament of the whole Church."

Just as Jesus was sent by the Father, says the constitution, so Christ sent the Apostles, filled with the Holy Spirit to preach the Gospel to every creature. They were to proclaim also that Jesus by His death and resurrection had freed us from the power of Satan and from death, and thus brought us into the kingdom of His Father. The Apostles were to accomplish the work of salvation by means of sacrifice and sacraments, "around which the entire liturgical life revolves."

By baptism, the constitution explains, men are plunged into the paschal mystery of Christ. They die with Him and rise with Him; they receive the spirit of adoption of sons, whereby they cry: "Abba, Father" (Rom. 8:15), and thus become true adorers whom the Father seeks. As frequently as they partake of the Lord's Supper, they proclaim the death of the Lord until He comes. Hence on the very day of Pentecost when the missionary Church appeared before the world, those who received the word of Peter were baptized.

The new Christians "continued steadfastly in the teaching of the Apostles and in the communion of the breaking of bread and in prayer . . . praising God and being in favor with all the people" (Acts 2:41-47). From that day the people of God have never failed to come together to celebrate the paschal mystery, reading those things "which were in all the Scriptures concerning him" (Lk. 24:27), and celebrating the Eucharist in which the victory and triumph of His death are again made present. At the same

time they gave "thanks to God for his unspeakable gift" (2 Cor.
9:15) "in Christ Jesus in praise of his glory" (Eph. 1:12), through
the power of the Holy Spirit.

How is the Church to continue Christ's redemptive work?
Christ, replies the constitution, is constantly present in the Church
and especially in her liturgical actions. He is present not only in
the sacrifice of the Mass but also and especially in the holy Eucharist. He is present and operative in the sacraments and in His word
so that it is He Himself who speaks when the holy Scriptures are
read. Lastly He is present when the people of God pray and sing,
for He promised: "Where two or three are gathered together in
my name, there am I in the midst of them" (Mt. 18:20).

What the Liturgy Really Is

Hence the liturgy is really the exercise of the priestly office of Jesus
Christ, wherein the sanctification of man is indicated by signs
visible to the senses and is achieved in a manner which corresponds
with each of these signs. In the liturgy the whole public worship is
enacted by the Mystical Body of Christ, embracing both the head
and the members. In consequence every liturgical celebration is
an act of Christ the priest and of His body, the Church; from this
it is evident that no other action of the Church can equal its
efficacy.

By participating in the liturgy we experience a foretaste of the
heavenly worship where Christ is sitting at the right hand of God,
a minister of the holies and of the true tabernacle. With all the
members of the celestial choir we sing a hymn to the Lord's glory.
In venerating the memory of the saints, we hope to have fellowship
with them. We eagerly look forward to the day when the Lord
Jesus Christ will come and we shall join Him in glory.

The constitution points out that before men can participate in
the liturgy they must receive the grace of faith. It quotes the words
of St. Paul to the Romans: "How then are they to call upon him
in whom they have not yet believed? But how are they to believe
him whom they have not heard? And how are they to hear if no
one preaches? And how are men to preach unless they be sent?"
(10:14–15).

Accordingly the Church proclaims the good news of salvation to unbelievers so that all men may know the true God and Jesus Christ whom He has sent, and may be converted from the error of their ways. To her own members the Church must preach faith and penance. She must prepare them for the sacraments, the observance of all of Christ's commandments, and the apostolate of piety and charity so they will be the light of the world and thus glorify the Father before men.

"Nevertheless," says the constitution, "the liturgy is the summit toward which the activity of the Church is directed; at the same time it is the fount from which all her power flows." The true object of the whole apostolate is to bring together all who have become sons of God by faith and Baptism to praise God in the midst of the Church, to participate in the Eucharistic sacrifice and to eat the Lord's supper.

Liturgy Nourishes the Faithful

In its turn the liturgy nourishes the faithful with the paschal sacraments, strengthens their faith, draws them into the ardent love of Christ and sets them on fire. "From the liturgy, therefore," says the constitution, "and especially from the Eucharist as from a fount, grace is poured forth on us; and the sanctification of men in Christ and the glorification of God, to which all other activities of the Church are directed as toward their end, is achieved in the most efficacious possible way."

Does the liturgy sanctify men automatically, without requiring any response on their part? No, replies the constitution, the faithful must come with the proper dispositions, their internal sentiments must harmonize with their voices and they must cooperate with divine grace to make it fruitful. Hence shepherds of souls must realize that the mere observance of the laws governing valid and licit celebration is not sufficient. They must prepare the faithful to participate intelligently and devoutly in the sacred rites.

Important as the liturgy is, it does not comprise man's whole spiritual life. The Christian should pray at times to the Father in secret; at other times he should pray with his brethren, and he should learn to make his whole day's work a prayer by dedicating it all to God. The spiritual life calls also for sacrifice and self-denial; by bearing about in our body the dying of Jesus, the life also of Jesus will be manifest in our bodily frame.

Moreover popular devotions are to be encouraged, provided they are in harmony with the laws and norms of the Church, and especially when they are ordered by the Holy See. Devotions proper to individual churches are likewise to be commended if they are undertaken at the request of the bishops or are sanctioned by long-established custom. All these devotions should be so arranged, however, that they harmonize with the liturgical seasons, accord with the liturgy and are in some fashion derived from it. Indeed they should lead the faithful to the liturgy, which by its very nature surpasses any of them.

The Participation of the Faithful

The constitution then discusses the promotion of liturgical instruction and active participation. The Church, it says, wants all the faithful to participate actively, intelligently and devoutly in liturgical celebrations. Such participation by the people of God is both their right and duty by virtue of their baptism, and it is the primary and indispensable source from which they derive the true Christian spirit. Hence shepherds of souls should provide the faithful with the necessary instruction. This is one of their most important duties. The constitution then sets forth the decrees enacted by the Council to provide for the proper instruction of seminarians, priests and religious by liturgical experts.

The Church, points out the constitution, is undertaking with great care a general restoration of the liturgy. This consists of immutable elements divinely instituted and of those subject to change. The latter may be revised if, with the passage of time, they have suffered from the addition of anything out of harmony with the inner nature of the liturgy or have become unsuited to it.

In such restoration both texts and rites should be arranged so that they manifest more clearly the holy things which they signify. The faithful should be enabled to understand them with ease and to take part in them fully, actively and as befits a community. The regulation of the liturgy belongs primarily to the Apostolic See, which concedes some authority to the bishop and, within defined limits, to various kinds of territorial conferences of bishops.

Any revision of the liturgy is to be preceded by careful theological, historical and pastoral research as well as by a study of the general laws governing the structure and meaning of the liturgy. The aim must be to retain sound tradition but keep the way open to legitimate progress. Any innovations should in some way grow organically from forms already existing. Furthermore care should be taken to avoid, as far as possible, notable differences between the rites in adjacent regions.

The Important Role of Scripture

The constitution stresses the important role of sacred Scripture in the celebration of the liturgy. It is from Holy Writ that the lessons are read and explained in the homilies, and the psalms are sung. The prayers, collects and liturgical songs are inspired by the Bible and it is from that holy book that actions and signs derive their meaning. Hence it is essential to foster a love for Scripture in order to achieve the restoration, progress and adaptation of the liturgy.

The constitution next outlines several principles drawn from the hierarchic and communal nature of the liturgy. It begins by pointing out that liturgical services are not private undertakings but are celebrations of the Church, which is "the sacrament of unity"—the people of God united under their bishops. Hence liturgical services both manifest and affect the whole body of the Church.

Whenever rites provide for communal celebration involving the presence and active participation of the faithful, this is generally to be preferred to an individual and quasi-private service. This applies with particular force to the celebration of the Mass and the administration of the sacraments, even though every Mass has of itself a public and social nature.

Each person, minister or layman, who has an office to perform, should do all of, but only, those parts which pertain to his office. Servers, lectors, commentators and choir members exercise genuine liturgical functions. Hence all should discharge their offices with sincere piety and decorum.

To foster active participation the faithful should be encouraged to take part by means of acclamations, responses, psalms, antiphons and hymns, as well as by actions, gestures and bodily attitudes. At proper times all should pray in reverent silence. The liturgy distinguishes between persons according to their liturgical offices and clerical rank, and liturgical laws provide for due honors to be accorded civil officials. Apart from such instances, no special honors are to be paid in the liturgy to private individuals or classes of persons, either in the ceremonies or by external display.

Liturgy: Didactic and Pastoral

The constitution next sets forth certain principles based upon the didactic and pastoral nature of the liturgy. It begins by pointing out that while the sacred liturgy is primarily the worship of the Divine Majesty, it nevertheless contains much instruction for the faithful. In the liturgy God speaks to the faithful and Christ proclaims His Gospel. By prayer and song the people reply to God.

Furthermore the prayers addressed to God by the celebrant who presides over the assembly in the person of Christ are recited in the name not only of the congregation present but also of the entire holy people of God. The visible symbols and signs used in the liturgy to signify invisible divine things have been selected by Christ or His Church. Hence the faith of the participants is nourished and their minds are lifted to God not only when things are read "which were written for our instruction" (Rom. 15:4), but also when the Church prays, sings or acts. In this way the faithful offer God their rational service and more abundantly receive His grace.

In the light of these considerations the following principles should be observed in the revision of the liturgy: "The rites should be distinguished by a noble simplicity; they should be short, clear and unencumbered by any useless repetitions; they should be within the people's powers of comprehension, and normally should not require much explanation."

Four Directives

That the intimate connection between words and rites may be evident in the liturgy, the constitution ordains:

(1) In sacred celebrations there is to be more reading from holy Scripture, and it is to be more varied and appropriate.

(2) The sermon is part of the liturgical service and the best place for it is to be indicated in the rubrics. It should draw its content mainly from Scriptural and liturgical sources. It should proclaim God's wonderful works in the history of salvation or in the mystery of Christ ever made present and active within us.

(3) Instruction of a more explicitly liturgical character should also be given; if necessary, short directives to be spoken by the priest or competent minister should be provided within the rites themselves.

(4) Bible services should be encouraged, especially on the vigils of the more solemn feasts, on some weekdays in Advent and Lent, and on Sundays and feast days.

While Latin still remains the official language in the Latin rites, the use of the mother tongue is frequently of great advantage to the faithful in the Mass, the administration of sacraments and other parts of the liturgy. Hence its use may be extended according to regulations specified by competent ecclesiastical authority.

Even in the liturgy, the constitution points out, the Church does not wish to impose a rigid uniformity in matters which do not involve the faith or the good of the whole community. She respects and fosters the genius and talents of the different races and nations and even admits things from their culture into the liturgy, provided they harmonize with its true and authentic spirit.

When revising the liturgical books, provision is to be made for legitimate variations and adaptations to diverse groups, regions and peoples, especially in the missions, provided that the substantial unity of the Roman rite is preserved. Within the limits set by the typical editions of the liturgical books, it belongs to competent ecclesiastical authority to specify adaptations of sacramentals, liturgical language, sacred music and the arts.

The Bishop: High Priest

The high priest of his flock, declares the constitution, is the bishop, from whom the life in Christ of his faithful is in some way derived. Hence all should hold in high esteem the liturgical life of the diocese centered around the bishop, especially in his cathedral.

Next comes the parish, in which the pastor takes the place of the bishop. The parishes represent the visible Church constituted throughout the world. As a consequence, the liturgical life of the parish and its relationship to the bishop must be fostered among the priests and the laity. Efforts should be made to encourage a sense of community within the parish, especially in the communal celebration of the Sunday Mass.

"Zeal for the promotion and restoration of the liturgy," says the constitution, "is rightly held to be a sign of the providential dispositions of God in our time, as a movement of the Holy Spirit in His Church. It is today a distinguishing mark of the Church's life, indeed of the whole tenor of contemporary religious thought and action."

To render even more vigorous such pastoral-liturgical action the Council decreed:

(1) Each territorial conference or assembly of bishops shall form a liturgical commission to be aided by experts in liturgical science, sacred music, art and pastoral practice. Under the guidance of ecclesiastical authority the commission is to regulate liturgical action throughout the territory and to promote studies and appropriate experiments whenever it appears that adaptations ought to be proposed to the Holy See.

(2) Every diocese is to establish a liturgical commission under the direction of the bishop to promote the liturgical apostolate.

(3) In addition to these liturgical commissions, every diocese should have commissions for sacred music and sacred art. Naturally these three commissions should work in the closest collaboration.

The Mystery of the Holy Eucharist

After presenting the general principles for the restoration and reform of the sacred liturgy, the constitution discusses the holy Eucharist, the great sacrament of Christ's undying love for men. "At the Last Supper," says the constitution, "on the night when He was betrayed, our Saviour instituted the Eucharistic sacrifice of His body and blood. He did this in order to perpetuate the sacrifice of the Cross throughout the centuries until He should come again; and He wished to entrust to His beloved spouse, the Church, a memorial of His death and resurrection, a sacrament of love, a sign of unity, a bond of charity, a paschal banquet in which

Christ is eaten, the mind is filled with grace and a pledge of future glory is given to us." Herein is found the doctrinal background for all that follows.

Echoing the notes sounded in *Mediator Dei* and the 1958 Instruction on Sacred Music and the Liturgy, the constitution expresses the Church's earnest desire that the faithful present at this mystery of faith should not be mere silent spectators but active participants thoroughly understanding the rites and prayers of the Mass. They should be enlightened by God's Word and nourished at the table of the Lord's body.

They should render thanks to God and join with the celebrant in offering the immaculate Victim as well as themselves to God. Thus they should be drawn, day by day, through Christ their Mediator, into ever more perfect union with God and with each other so that finally God may be all in all.

To achieve these ends more effectively the Council has decreed certain changes in the Masses which are celebrated with the assistance of the faithful, now commonly called the recitative Masses. The rite of the Mass is to be revised to bring out more clearly the intrinsic nature and purpose of its several parts and to enable the faithful to participate in it with greater devotion.

The rites are to be simplified and elements which, with the passage of time, come to be duplicated or were unwisely added, are to be discarded. Other elements, which suffered injury through accidents of history, are to be restored to the vigor which they had in the early centuries.

Noteworthy is the stress placed upon the greater use of Scripture. "The treasure of the Bible," the constitution prescribes, "are to be opened up more lavishly so that richer fare may be provided for the faithful at the table of God's word. In this way a more representative portion of the holy Scriptures will be read to the people in the course of a prescribed number of years."

The Importance of the Homily

The important and fruitful role of the homily is likewise stressed. It should explain the mysteries of the faith and the guiding principles of the Christian life during the course of the liturgical year.

Hence the homily is to be regarded as part of the liturgy itself and at Masses on Sundays and holy days of obligation is not to be omitted except for a serious reason.

On these days there is to be restored, after the Gospel with its homily, the Community Prayer or Prayer of the Faithful. The faithful are to participate in this prayer, in which intercession is made for the Church, civil authorities, the needy and for the salvation of the whole world.

In Masses celebrated with the faithful the mother tongue may be used in the readings and Prayer of the Faithful and in those items which pertain to the people. If a still greater use of the mother tongue is deemed desirable, permission may be secured from the proper ecclesiastical authority.

The constitution strongly commends the more perfect form of participating in the Mass whereby the faithful, after the celebrant's communion, receive the Lord's body from the same holy Sacrifice. The faithful receive the whole Christ, body and blood, soul and divinity, under the single species of the bread. But Communion under both species may be granted, when the bishops deem fit, not only to clerics but also to the laity.

Since the two parts of the Mass—the liturgy of the word and the Eucharistic liturgy—form but one single act of worship, the Council strongly urges pastors to explain to the faithful the importance of participating in the entire Mass, especially on Sundays and holy days of obligation. The constitution ends its discussion of the holy Eucharist by pointing out that the practice of concelebration, whereby the unity of the priesthood is appropriately manifested, has remained in use to this day in the Church. The Council has extended permission for concelebration to several occasions when a number of priests are assembled. A new rite for concelebration is to be drawn up and inserted into the Roman missal.

The Other Sacraments and Sacramentals

Before treating of the *other* sacraments the Council wisely devoted an entire chapter to the mystery of the holy Eucharist, that is to say, the Mass. It is the heart of the whole sacramental system. What the sun is to the planets in our solar system, the Mass is to the other

sacraments. Around it the others gravitate, and it holds them together in a marvelously balanced unity.

In the opening sentence of the chapter, the constitution sets forth
the purpose of the sacraments: "The purpose of the sacraments is to
sanctify men, to build up the body of Christ and finally to give
worship to God; because they are signs they also instruct."

It then cites their relationship to faith and their fruitfulness:
"They not only presuppose faith, but by words and objects they
also nourish, strengthen and express it; that is why they are called
'sacraments of faith.' They have indeed the power to impart grace
but, in addition, the very act of celebrating them effectively disposes
the faithful to receive grace fruitfully, to worship God duly and to
love each other mutually."

This beautiful exposition supplements the great stress placed by
the Council of Trent upon the intrinsic power of the rite to cause
grace *ex opere operato* and restores the proper balance between sign
and causality that was unfortunately often obscured in the post-Tridentine period. The constitution declares that it is "of the highest
importance that the faithful should easily understand the sacramental
signs." Because of this earnest desire of Vatican Council II, so explicitly stated in its *Constitution on the Sacred Liturgy,* we shall
treat this theme at length in subsequent chapters and shall show the
profound impact upon the whole sacramental system by the Council's carefully thought out document.

Indeed it is this earnest desire of the Council that has brought
into being not only in every diocese but also in almost every
parish the program of what is now called pastoral liturgy. The
Council Fathers expressed the conviction that the faithful will more
readily understand the sacraments if they have the "noble simplicity"
as prescribed in the new liturgy, and that they will frequent the
sacraments not simply out of a sense of obligation or because of
social pressures but eagerly and joyously.

Since the sacraments produce the graces which they signify, they
have Christ for their author and are beyond the power of the
Church to institute. The Church, however, does something analo-
gous: she institutes sacramentals. "These are sacred signs," the
Constitution explains, which bear a resemblance to the sacraments;
they signify spiritual effects which are to be obtained through the

Church's intercession. By their aid men are disposed to receive the chief fruits of the sacraments, and various occasions in daily life are rendered holy."

The Sacramentals Quicken Devotion

While the sacramentals are infinitely inferior to the sacraments, they nevertheless help maintain contact with the holy by elevating their thoughts and stirring their emotions. Hence it is, as the constitution shows, that the liturgy of the sacraments and sacramentals sanctifies almost every important event in the lives of the faithful. They are brought into life-giving contact with the stream of divine grace which flows from the paschal mystery of the passion, death and resurrection of Christ, the fount from which all sacraments and sacramentals draw their power.

During the past fifty years liturgy studies have shown how accretions, picked up like barnacles over the centuries, have tended to obscure the meaning of the sacraments and sacramentals, especially for the people of our own time. After candidly acknowledging the truth of the criticism, the constitution says: "Hence some changes have become necessary to adapt them to the needs of our own day."

Accordingly the Council enacted decrees concerning revisions to be made in each of the sacraments and with some of the sacramentals. The decrees are, however, general principles of reform rather than concrete proposals. The specific details of reform are to be worked out by post-conciliar commissions.

The revisions cover a wide range: a greater use of the vernacular in administering sacraments and sacramentals, a new rite for the baptism of infants and of adults, a clarification of the role of godparents, the formulas for the sacrament of penance, regulations for the anointing of the sick, and the enrichment of the nuptial rite to signify the graces of the sacraments, and the obligations of the spouses.

The sacramentals will be revised to enable the people to participate actively, easily and intelligently. Changes will be made so that some sacramentals, in special circumstances, may be administered by qualified lay persons. The Constitution also treats of the Divine

Office, the liturgical year, sacred music, sacred art and furnishings, and revision of the calendar—topics which are beyond the scope of this book. Because the Council wisely contented itself with the formulation of the general principles for the renewal of the liturgy, allowing each generation to apply them in the light of new and changed conditions, the constitution on the liturgy provides guidance for the maintenance of a well ordered, intelligent and fruitful liturgical life within the Church for many years to come.

V.
RENEWAL IN SACRAMENTAL THEOLOGY

THERE are few, if any, areas of the Church's teaching and practice, in which renewal has been more clearly marked than in that of the sacraments. For many centuries Christians have received the sacraments as though the graces flowing from them were the recipient's exclusive personal possession and had little reference to anyone save God and himself. The ancient Christian tradition that the sacraments have profound social and churchly implications has been almost entirely obscured by the attitude of spiritual individualism which has so long prevailed.

This *laissez-faire* spirituality has been further strengthened by emphasizing the automatic efficacy of the sacraments and minimizing the role of the recipient. To many people the sacraments operate like automatic vending machines. Put a coin in the machine and out comes your cup of coffee or piece of pie. As long as the external action is properly performed, the product comes out automatically, regardless of the dispositions of the recipient.

The sacraments have come to be viewed by all too many as *things* rather than as the *actions* or *gestures* of Christ. They operate like machines and "deliver the goods," provided the proper *matter* and *form* are used. These guarantee not only the validity of the sacraments but their fruitfulness if no obstacle is placed in their way.

Such a view has been reinforced by the emphasis placed upon the *ex opere operato* aspects of the sacrament's efficacy. This famous phrase was first used by Peter of Poitiers, a Chancellor of the University of Paris in the twelfth century (1170–75). Adopted by theologians generally, the phrase literally means "from the work done, effected or brought about."

It was used by the Council of Trent (1545–63) to signify the grace produced by the sacramental rite itself. It stresses the fact that grace is a gift of God and is not earned by the effort of the minister or of the recipient. Thus when the sacramental rite is validly performed with the proper intention, grace and other supernatural gifts are conferred on the willing recipient by the objective application of the external sacramental sign.

This one-sided stress on the causality of the external sacramental rite, independent of the internal acts and dispositions of both the minister and the recipient, has contributed greatly to the mechanistic view of the sacraments just outlined. "Despite all our protestations to the contrary," says Father Diekmann, "such a view sounds like magic. And there can be no doubt that, in practice, sacraments were regarded in this mechanistic fashion by vast sections of the faithful before the Reformation. Superstitious uses of sacraments abounded. To all intents and purposes, they *were* medicine chests. The Protestant accusation that sacraments are a man-made machinery interposed between Christ and the soul, the Protestant revolt against sacramentalism, and their appeal for a personal religion, a religion of personal union with Christ, could not have found a willing audience otherwise. Luther's denunciations of the *ex opere operato* were justified if we recognize how that term was then widely understood, and, I'm afraid, how not a few of our people understand it today."

How did such a one-sided and unbalanced idea of the sacraments come into being and become so widespread among the faithful? How does the renewal and reform movement restore the Church's teaching to its proper balance? To answer these questions we shall sketch in the following chapters the meaning and history of the sacraments, the relation of sign and causality, the presence and redeeming activity of Christ in the sacraments, the personal encounter with Christ, the role of faith and the importance of the recipient's response in the dialog with Christ. Then we shall discuss the two inspiring themes which the modern theological renewal stresses so much: Christ as the Primordial Sacrament of God and the Church as the basic sacrament of Christ.

Sacraments: Their Meaning and History

First of all, it should be pointed out that almighty God can and does give grace in answer to the prayers and needs of men without the use of an external sign or ceremony. This is evident from the fact that God, grace and the soul are spiritual realities. But it is evident from the Bible that God has been pleased to use visible signs and ceremonies as the channels through which certain blessings and graces have been conferred upon man.

This is a gracious recognition by the Creator of the twofold nature of man, spiritual and corporeal. Much of his knowledge is acquired through the use of his senses, and God accordingly makes use of external signs and ceremonies in his communicating and sanctifying relations with man.

In the broadest sense of the word a sacrament is the sign of something sacred and hidden. In this sense the whole universe may be said to be a vast sacramental system inasmuch as visible things serve as the signs of things invisible and sacred, even of the Godhead. It was in this sense that the Psalmist proclaimed: "The heavens show forth the glory of God, and the firmament declareth the work of his hands" (Ps. 18:2). This too was the basic truth which the Apostle Paul announced: "The invisible things of him [God], from the creation of the world, are clearly seen, being understood by the things that are made" (Rom. 1:20).

The crowning evidence of God's desire to deal with man in the manner best suited to his corporeal and spiritual natures is the Incarnation. This tremendous mystery and the greatest event in the history of the world—God taking on man's nature and becoming flesh and blood—may be said to be the Mystery of mysteries and the Sacrament of sacraments. Contrasting this stupendous reality with the figures and types of the Old Testament, St. Paul says: "So we too, when we were children, were enslaved under the elements of the world. But when the fulness of time came, God sent His Son, born of a woman, born under the Law, that he might redeem those under the Law, that we might receive the adoption of sons" (Gal. 4:3–5).

External signs and symbols of God's omnipotence and infinite perfections become truly sacramental only when they convey to us a participation in His holiness and in His divine life. They confer upon the recipient sanctifying grace and thus restore him to the supernatural order lost by the fall of our first parents. Hence St. Thomas Aquinas defined a sacrament simply as "the sign of a sacred thing in so far as it sanctifies men."

The Catechism of the Council of Trent defines it as something visible to the senses, which by divine institution has the power both to signify and to effect sanctity and justice. Catechisms in English have generally defined the sacrament as "an outward sign of inward grace" or as "a sacred and mysterious sign or ceremony, ordained by Christ, by which grace is conveyed to our souls." The latter two definitions bring out clearly the three things necessary for a sacrament: outward sign, inward grace and divine institution.

The Involvement of Christ and Church

Bringing out more explicitly the involvement of Christ and the Church in every sacrament is the definition formulated by the *Catholic Encyclopedia for School and Home:* "A sacrament is an external act of worship by which Christ, through His Church and minister, representing the mysteries of His life, signifies and produces through the rite itself the sanctification of a man who has the right disposition."

A still more comprehensive definition, which reflects the developments of modern theological thought, is given by Matthew J. O'Connell, S.J., in *Thought* magazine: "A sacrament is a symbolic action whereby Christ continues in and through His Church the perfect cult of His earthly mysteries and whereby He sanctifies His members, configuring them to Himself and by that very fact dynamically ordering them to the fulfillment of salvation in the vision of God."

The theological research of the 1960's has provided us with insights into elements such as personal encounter, the churchly dimension and worship, which had not received proper attention in previous attempts to describe the sacraments. These insights are reflected in Vatican Council II's *Constitution on the Sacred Liturgy,* which redresses, as we shall show later, the imbalance between sign and causality.

In his scholarly work, *Theology of the Sacraments,* Pierre Pourrat points out that "in the first four centuries the Church administered the sacraments without theorizing about them." Although the Fathers of the Church in those early centuries did not attempt to work out a technical theology of the sacraments, they made transparently clear in their sermons and writings the essential nature and fruitfulness of the sacraments. Speaking of baptism, Tertullian (d. 230) said: "The Holy Spirit comes down from heaven and hovers over the waters, sanctifying them of Himself and thus they imbibe the power of sanctifying." St. Augustine, Bishop of Hippo (d. 430), was the first to attempt a technical definition: "a sacrament is a sign of grace."

It was not until the twelfth century, however, that serious efforts were made to formulate a theology of the sacraments. Peter the Lombard (d. 1160) in his famous *Summa Sententiarum* formulated the principles which clearly distinguish the seven sacraments from the numerous minor signs which henceforth were to be known as sacramentals. It remained for St. Thomas (d. 1274), however, to work out the first systematic treatment of the theology of the sacraments. He completed St. Augustine's definition of a sacrament by adding the idea that it is an *efficacious* sign of grace.

His distinctive contribution is his exposition of the manner in which the sacraments are instrumental causes deriving their efficacy from the passion and death of Christ. In his exposition the emphases upon sign and causality are beautifully balanced. During the last seven centuries theological interest has unfortunately been focused chiefly upon causality.

In his book *The Theological Dimensions of the Liturgy,* Cyprian Vagaggini points out that theology after St. Thomas "and especially since the sixteenth century, in the treatment of the sacraments in general and in particular, has so relegated the concept of sign to second place that it has, practically speaking, forgotten it or, at least, has left it inoperative." In his bitterly polemical *De Captivitate Babylonica,* Martin Luther describes what the Church and its sacramental system had become in the eyes of many at that time. He says that the image projected by the Church was substantially that of "an enormous pumping machine" supposed to enable its members to draw upon the merits of Christ and the saints, and for this purpose ending in seven large taps. At each one of these taps stands a priest, ready to turn the spigot so that it will give a few drops every time a customer comes and pays the price.

A Spiritual Supermarket?

This is, of course, a gross caricature. "But," asks Louis Bouyer in his penetrating study, *The Sacramental System,* "is there some trace in it of what we do to the sacraments through our too facile description of them as seven parallel channels distributing grace to mankind by the ministration of the priests? Is this more or less how they appear in the routine of our daily practice?"

Answering his own queries, he says: "I think the best which can be said is that to the average Christian the Church with its seven sacraments appears as a kind of big spiritual supermarket or cafeteria. As he sees it, there are seven different counters to which he may go to fulfill his various needs. Then he has only to choose what is needed, with the help of the competent assistant, and after that to 'cash and carry'! Whether he will consume the goods provided for him on the spot or at home, nobody has a right to care."

Bouyer points out that the Christian who entertains such a notion fails to perceive that the sacramental system is an organic whole and that the Church is vastly more than just an organization catering to the sustenance of the individual's life. He fails to realize that the Church is a living organism in which the Christian life is vitalized and nurtured in *community.*

To understand how Luther could picture the Church and her sacramental system as a huge pumping machine rendering a service similar to that now performed by a food vending instrument with seven outlets, it is necessary to recall the fierce attacks launched against the Church by the Reformers and the Church's reaction to them. The Reformers generally held that the sacraments are signs of something sacred—grace and faith—but denied that they really cause divine grace.

Rejecting completely the *ex opere operato* aspect of the sacraments, Luther and his early followers regarded the sacraments as merely "signs and testimonies of God's good will to us" (Augsburg Confession). They excite faith, and this fiduciary type of faith causes justification. Substantially the same views are held by Calvinists and Presbyterians. Zwingli and his followers reduced the dignity of the sacraments still further by regarding them as signs not of God's fidelity but of our fidelity. We show our faith in Christ by receiving the sacraments, which are mere badges of our profession.

Basically these notions stemmed from Luther's newly formulated doctrine of justification by faith alone. Man is sanctified not by an inward renovation through grace which washes away his sins but by an extrinsic imputation through the merits of Christ, which covers his soul as a cloak. Hence there is no place for signs which *generate* grace; their only purpose is to *excite* faith in the Saviour. Such were the doctrines being proclaimed by the innovators in many parts of Christendom, and winning vast numbers from the ancient faith, when the Council of Trent opened on December 13, 1545.

Traditional Teaching Confirmed

Condemning the new doctrines, the Council declared: "If anyone say that the sacraments of the New Law do not contain the grace which they signify, or that they do not confer grace on those who place no obstacle to the same, let him be anathema. . . . If anyone say that grace is not conferred by the sacraments *ex opere operato,* but that faith in God's promises is alone sufficient for obtaining grace, let him be anathema. . . ." Here were uncompromising reaffirmations of the traditional teaching and blunt condemnations of the new doctrines. The whole atmosphere was one of heated controversy and passionate polemics. Shortage of time and the turbulent period during which the Council was held prevented it from undertaking the development of the positive aspects of the sacraments.

The prickly burr of controversy is an inept spur toward working out a balanced theology. Excessive stress on certain phases is likely to lead to the neglect or minimizing of others. "One can never satisfactorily define the Catholic thesis," as Denis O'Callaghan remarks, "in terms of the antithesis."

The powerful influence of the cultural and religious climate of the day upon the direction of theological thought is strikingly illustrated by a recent occurrence. On the day I write these lines there comes to my desk a copy of the English edition of *Justification* by Hans Küng. This is the famous doctoral thesis in which Küng undertakes a critical analysis of Barth's *Dogmatics,* especially volume IV, on the meaning of justification. He then compares Barth's interpretation with that of the Catholic Church and finds substantial agreement, tracing the apparent differences to semantic misunderstandings. The volume is published with an *imprimatur*.

The incident shows the powerful influence of the ecumenical spirit in fostering friendship and understanding and in prompting theologians of both sides to find interpretations favorable to Christian unity. A climate that was the direct opposite of this obtained at the time of the Council of Trent, when the reformers and Counter-Reformers were at swords' points.

It must be frankly acknowledged, however, that the Council of Trent rendered an invaluable service in safeguarding the traditional Christian belief in the objective efficacy of the sacraments in serving as channels of divine grace to those who place no obstacle in its way. Neither did the Council deny that the sacraments have among their purposes the stimulating and nourishing of the faith of the recipients. This is evident from the wording of the Council's decree: "If anyone shall say that the sacraments were instituted *only* for the purpose of nourishing faith, let him be anathema."

It is unfortunate, however, that the Council's chief objective of shoring up the Church's defenses against the attacks of the reformers, with their exaggerated emphasis upon faith alone, kept her theologians from exploring and explicating the admission implicit in the word *only*. It is understandable too how they turned to the baptism of infants to clinch their thesis concerning the *ex opere operato* effects of the sacraments. Here the dispositions of the recipient are at a minimum and recourse is had to those of the sponsors and to the faith of the Church.

Balance Restored

This tended to depict the sacrament not as the saving action of Christ but as an impersonal, mechanical thing. It led one to imagine, as Denis O'Callaghan points out, "that there were 'two ways' of salvation, namely, personal and sacramental holiness. But as Scripture constantly teaches, justification is achieved by the inner unity of faith *and* sacrament." It is true that this impression could be corrected by a careful study of the wording of the decrees and of the statement of doctrine, but few undertook this task. Furthermore it should not be necessary if the doctrinal emphasis were not so badly out of balance.

The balance is happily restored by the constitution on the liturgy issued by the Second Vatican Council, which says: "The sacraments are ordained to the sanctification of men, to the building up of the body of Christ, to the worship of God; as signs also they have a place in instruction. They not only presuppose faith, but they nourish, strengthen and express it by word and action; therefore are they called the sacraments of faith. They do indeed confer grace, but their celebration disposes the faithful most efficaciously for a fruitful reception, for the worship of God, and for the exercise of charity."

Here is a beautiful and delicate balancing of emphases upon sign and causality, as well as a recognition of the important role of faith and of the nourishing and deepening effect of the sacraments upon it. Here is a wondrous recapturing and renewal of the authentic faith of the Christian body from the time of the Apostles to the present. The sacraments are not lifeless mechanical things: they are living signs of our faith and of Christ's redeeming love. They are the saving actions of Christ flooding us with His divine life, grace and love.

"They are," as John H. Miller shows in his stimulating work, *Signs of Transformation in Christ,* "the unique source of our salvation and sanctification. They alone make us like to Christ, God's only Son; they alone make us over into Christ, for they alone make us participate in His life."

The expressive phrase "sacraments of faith" was repeatedly used by St. Thomas—fifteen times in his discussion of baptism alone—

and by other theologians up to the Council of Trent. But with Luther's banner *Sola fides* then so prominent on the European horizon, they avoided this phrase. It was a pity that necessity compelled them to do so, for the phrase emphasizes the all-important truth that the sacraments are essentially expressions of the living faith and worship of the Mystical Body, which give them their true significance as symbolic actions.

Furthermore the phrase articulates the initial response of the recipient which the inherent power of the sacrament, as an act of Christ, perfects. The increasing use of the phrase "sacraments of faith" in recent years is a powerful help to theologians in removing the erroneous impression of not a few that the sacraments provide an easy way to salvation, requiring merely that the recipient place no obstacle to their inherent efficacy.

Sacraments: Actions of Christ

Leaders in the renewal of sacramental theology are now depicting the sacraments not so much as "things" which we receive, but as the continuation and fulfillment of Christ's redemptive activities. They are the actions of Christ, by which we are lifted up into Himself and into the redeemed community, wherein we are united with His supreme objective of rendering praise and homage to the eternal and transcendent God.

The renewal does not stop, however, with the redemptive presence and activity of Christ in the sacraments. It goes on to explore the nature of that reality in greater detail and reaches the conclusion that the sacraments secure their results by causing us to *re-enact,* in a mystical manner, the redemptive drama of our divine Saviour. Thus the sacraments do more than share Christ's life with us and provide us with the grace of adoption.

Expressing the conclusion of these leaders, Father Diekmann, himself one of our foremost authorities, says: "We are saved not just by the application of Christ's saving grace to us, not just by the extension of His life to us. We are saved, basically, by being baptized, dipped, into the passion and resurrection of Christ. In the sacrament He unites us to the *source* of His saving grace. In the real sense of the word, we are saved in Christ's passion and resurrection: in His dying and rising. What happened to our head, really and physically, now happens to us really though sacramentally."

This concept brings out vividly not only the presence of Christ in the sacrament but also His power and dynamism in redeeming us here and now by uniting us to His death and resurrection, which are actualized anew in us. It throws into clear relief the central truth of Christianity that the passion, death and resurrection of the divine Redeemer extend to men in every generation and thus enable them to die to the old Adam and live the life of the new Adam, Jesus Christ, our Lord and King.

The Threefold Significance of the Sacraments

This view reflects beautifully the teaching of St. Thomas concerning the threefold significance of each sacrament. (1) As a commemorative sign of what has gone before, it signifies Christ's passion, death and resurrection and thus points to the source of our sanctification. "All we who have been baptized into Christ Jesus," says St. Paul, "have been baptized into his death" (Rom. 6:3). (2) As a demonstrative sign of what is being wrought in us through the death and resurrection of Christ, it confers sacramental grace. "For we were buried with him," continues the Apostle, "by means of baptism" (Rom. 6:4). (3) As a prognostic or prophetic sign, it is the pledge of eternal life. "For if," concludes St. Paul, "we have been united with him in the likeness of his death, we shall be so in the likeness of his resurrection also (Rom. 6:5).

This renewal of sacramental theology brings to the fore the teachings of St. Thomas, who did such a superb job of connecting the sacraments with the life of Christ, especially His passion, death and resurrection, and thus gives new vitality and contemporary relevance to them. In his masterly work, *A Key to the Doctrine of the Eucharist,* Dom Anscar Vonier comments with keen insight upon the Angelic Doctor's exposition of the threefold significance of the sacraments and elucidates it. In pleasant contrast to some theological writers who employ a nebulous verbosity which exhausts one's patience and wearies his spirit, Vonier expresses himself with crystal clarity and simplicity, which make him a joy to read.

"Every sacrament, then," he says, "announces something: it brings back the past, it is the voice of the present, it reveals the future. If the sacrament did no longer proclaim as a sign something which is not seen, it would not be a sacrament. In every sacrament there is a past, a present and a future: the death of Christ is its past; supernatural transformation is its present; eternal glory is its future. It can embrace heaven and earth, time and eternity, because it is a sign. Were it only a grace, it would be no more than the gift of the present hour; but being a sign the whole history of the spiritual world is reflected in it."

This is illustrated in the memorable words of our Lord, as quoted by St. Paul in his First Letter to the Corinthians: "This cup is the new testament in my blood; do this as often as you drink it, in remembrance of me. For as often as you shall eat this bread and drink the cup, you proclaim the death of the Lord, until he comes" (11:25–26). Thus does the sacrament of the Eucharist, instituted at the Last Supper and re-enacted at every altar today, continue to show forth the death of the Lord until He comes. The threefold sign of the past, present and future is thus woven into the Eucharist as it is into each of the other sacraments.

Shift in Emphasis

The renewal in sacramental theology shifts the emphasis from the matter, ceremony and words used in a sacrament, as causes of grace, to the dynamic presence of Christ and to His redeeming and sanctifying activity in the sacrament. The correction of this malfocus removes the danger of construing the sacraments as a form of magic or the operations of a vending machine.

Since the sacraments are personal acts of Christ, they derive their efficacy from Him and His redeeming passion, death and resurrection. This makes the whole sacramental system Christ-centered and helps the recipient to remember that in the sacraments Christ is not only speaking to him but also pouring out His grace and love in a personal encounter.

Hence the theological renewal helps all to see how unfounded are the charges of superficial critics who say the sacraments are only rites consisting of material things and words—a mere refinement of the abracadabra of the magician and the medicine man. They fail to see that it is the power behind the words, and not merely the words themselves, which determine their efficacy. Take water, for example. By itself it will not generate light; but put the power and skill of an engineer behind it, and he will harness it and cause it to generate power and light for an entire city or even for whole states. Take a piece of paper. Put on it the signatures of honorable men and it will spell the difference between war and peace, between world slaughter and world friendship.

Take a word. Put the power of a poet behind it and it will make music, beauty and cadence and will sing in the hearts of men. Put the power of an orator behind it and it will thrill multitudes. Put the power of a judge behind it and it spells the difference between legal innocence and guilt, between freedom and jail, between life and death. Put the power of God behind it and it pulls a universe into being out of the yawning abyss of nothingness.

Take a piece of bread. Put the power of a human being behind it and it is transformed by metabolic action into his own flesh and blood. Put the power of God, expressed in a few words, behind it and it is transformed into the body and blood, soul and divinity of our glorified Lord and Saviour, Jesus Christ.

What is determinative, decisive and all important is not so much the word as it is the *power behind* the word. When infinite power and intelligence are put behind a word it becomes the plenipotentiary ambassador of the Most High, clothed with a divine efficacy which transcends the power of man as the radiance of the sun surpasses the flickering light of a candle. God and a word can cause a universe to spring into being. God and a word can bring our great High Priest, Calvary's Victim for the sins of man, Jesus Christ, upon our altar under the lowly species of bread and wine.

Behind the words of the minister of each sacrament is the infinite power of the God-man, Jesus Christ, who echoes the words of the minister and acts through him. The same immeasurable might, which astounded the spectators when Jesus by His word cleansed the lepers, restored sight to the blind and hearing to the deaf and called forth the dead Lazarus from the tomb, is operative in the sacraments.

When Christ said to the paralytic who was let down from the roof, "Son, thy sins are forgiven thee," the Scribes scoffingly said:

"He blasphemes. Who can forgive sins, but God only?" Then to show them that He possessed such power, He said to the paralytic: "Arise, take up thy pallet, and go to thy house." When the scoffers witnessed such a display of power, "they were all amazed, and glorified God, saying, 'Never did we see the like'" (Mk. 2:5-12).

Sacraments Are Signs of Faith

In the sacraments the infinite might of the God-man is working similar miracles but we see them only with the eyes of faith. Faith is basic in the operation of all the sacraments. St. Thomas never tires of calling them "signs of faith" and "signs proclaiming or expressing faith." The sacraments are signs or acts of faith not only of the individual recipient but also of the Church. It is faith that moves mountains, works each day unseen miracles and lies at the root of all justification. Without faith the sacraments become but empty signs and hollow symbols.

"The clearer we see in faith," says the *Catholic Encyclopedia for School and Home,* "the greater our opportunity for union with God in sacramental encounters. As they are signs of our sanctification, the sacraments are also signs of our worship as well as Christ's. In them is expressed our sincere surrender in faith and love, and in proportion to the sincerity of this inner worship does our outward manifestation in sacramental signs, insofar as it is our act, become authentic."

This stress upon faith brings out vividly the importance and necessity of the *response* of the individual in the sacramental encounter with Christ. The sacraments, as Father Palmer says, "can neither save nor sanctify unless there is a personal response of faith, hope and love on the part of the knowing recipient. . . . The individual Christian is called upon to join Christ in the community of the faithful in offering a communal, social and ever-expanding hymn of praise to God. In doing so his personality is not suppressed or absorbed by the community; rather he is called to the highest form of self-expression, a self which becomes ever more identified with Christ in His mystical community."

This is the emphasis which the modern theological renewal is happily placing upon faith and the dynamic presence of Christ and

His sanctifying and redeeming activity in the sacraments, thus making their reception moving personal encounters with Christ. If these crucially important truths concerning the sacraments, along with the clarifying statement on the relation of faith to justification had been properly promulgated, preached and explained in the decades before the Reformation, one may well wonder whether the movement that shattered the unity of Christendom might not have been averted.

VI.

CHRIST: THE SACRAMENT OF GOD

In recent years the theology of the sacraments has achieved new depth, meaning and insight through its development of the great germinal truth first expressed by St. Augustine in the fifth century: "There is no other sacrament of God than Christ." As the effective sign of God's redeeming grace and love, Christ is the great primeval sacrament of God. He is the supreme sign of God, the visible Incarnation of His love and the pledge of our redemption.

In speaking of Jesus as the sacrament of God we are, of course, referring to Our Lord in His human nature, which He shares with us and in which He was visible to man. In referring to Him in His human nature we do not imply that He ceases to be divine. Indeed it is the divine personality hypostatically united to His human nature that gives to His redeeming activity its infinite worth and merit. It was through the God-man, Jesus Christ, that almighty God made His sacramental encounter with man.

It was to enable man to make that encounter that the Eternal Word took our flesh and dwelt among us. This stupendous mystery of the Incarnation is the central message of all the writers of the New Testament. In the prologue to his Gospel St. John tells us that no one has at any time seen God but "the only-begotten Son, who is in the bosom of the Father, he has revealed him." How did He reveal Him? How did He show us the mind and heart of God and enable us to meet Him?

Christ did this by becoming man. "And the Word," says the Evangelist John, "was made flesh and dwelt among us. And we saw his glory—glory of the only-begotten of the Father—full of grace and of truth . . . and of his fullness we have all received, grace for grace" (1:14–18).

KANSAS SCHOOL OF RELIGION
UNIVERSITY OF KANSAS
1300 OREAD AVENUE
LAWRENCE, KANSAS 66044

While Yahweh favored the Hebrew people by rescuing them from the bondage of the Egyptians and leading them by a cloud by day and a pillar of fire by night, He bestowed upon mankind an infinitely greater gift when He gave them His divine Son, our Incarnate Lord and God. Flesh of our flesh and blood of our blood, Jesus is man's link with the Almighty Creator. He is God's love incarnate, His greatest gift and His "primordial sacrament."

Christ: the Primordial Sacrament

This is the term preferred by Edward Schillebeeckx of Nijmegen University, Holland, the Dominican theologian who, along with Karl Rahner, has been chiefly responsible for reviving the original Biblical and patristic concept of a sacrament as a personal encounter with Christ. In his penetrating and profound work, *Christ the Sacrament of the Encounter with God,* he says: "If the human love and all the human acts of Jesus possess a divine saving power, then the realization in human shape of this saving power necessarily includes as one of its aspects the manifestation of salvation: includes, in other words, sacramentality. The man Jesus, as the personal visible realization of the divine grace of baptism, is *the* sacrament, the primordial sacrament, because this man, the Son of God himself, is intended by the Father to be in his humanity the only way to the actuality of redemption."

Like every true sacrament Christ not only symbolizes God's love but also conveys it to us. In so doing He does more in making God known to us than all the philosophers and theologians of all the ages. How so? Because Jesus in His own person manifests the love of God as no book could ever reveal it to us, and in exhibiting that love our Lord discloses the very essence and the inmost nature and being of the inscrutable and eternal God, which are infinite love. That is the reason why theologians who have thought, studied and meditated deeply upon this feel compelled to call Christ the Primordial Sacrament of God.

In his stimulating book, *Pathways to the Reality of God,* Rufus Jones tells of a little boy who was being put to bed by his mother. Kissing him, she said, "Good night, Johnny. Sleep tight." Then she turned out the light and started for the door. A sudden fear came over the child as the darkness closed in on him.

"Am I to be left all alone, Mommy," he asked, "and in the dark too?"

"Yes, my dear," replied the mother. "But you know you have God with you all the time."

"Yes, I know God is here," said the boy, "but I want someone who has a face."

Such too is the anxious, wistful cry of men and women everywhere. "We know in the abstract," observes Rufus Jones, "that God is Mind and Spirit and that He is near us. But we want to have a more vivid sense of His reality and His presence in our world, and above all, we want to see Him and to discover Him as a real Person with an actual Life and Character." This is precisely what Jesus does for us. It is in Him that we see not only the face of God but also His personal character.

That God-intoxicated man, the Beloved Disciple, who was privileged to rest His head upon the bosom of the Divine Master and to hear the throbbing of His Sacred Heart drives this basic truth home to us in language so simple that even a child can understand. "Beloved," he says, "let us love one another, for love is from God. And everyone who loves is born of God, and knows God. He who does not love does not know God; for God is love. In this has the love of God been shown in our case, that God has sent his only-begotten Son into the world that we may live through him. In this is the love, not that we have loved God, but that he has first loved us, and sent his Son a propitiation for our sins. Beloved, if God has so loved us, we also ought to love one another" (1 Jn. 4:7-11).

What philosopher or theologian has ever given us such a penetrating definition of God as has the Beloved Disciple in the three simple words "God is love"? Who has manifested that love to us so clearly, impressively and eloquently as the Christ who became the incarnation of that love and in that incarnate bodily form died for love of us on Calvary's Cross?

Standing on the mountain peak between the vast eternities of time and space, Jesus Christ is God's visible intervention into time and history. In the person of Christ God invades time to lift man into supernatural union with Himself, giving man his first contact with the eternal and infinite Godhead. Through the person of His divine Son, God floods man's soul with His divine life, grace and love. He thus makes Christ not only the link between earth and heaven, between time and eternity, but also the primordial foundation Sacrament, the *Ursakrament* (root-sacrament)—the term German theologians are fond of using—from which our seven sacraments derive their efficacy. They are but extensions of the sacramentality of Christ. Severed from the paschal mystery of His redeeming passion, death, resurrection and ascension, they would be but empty signs and tinkling cymbals.

Personal Encounters with Christ

It is obvious that this concept of Christ as the sacrament of God adds new dimensions of depth and meaning to sacramental theology. It brings out the important fact that sacramentality is the very heart of God's plan of salvation. When the Christian perceives that the sacraments are personal encounters with Christ, present and operative in each, there is little likelihood that he will approach them as automatic vending machines, dispensing salvation *ex opere operato* to those not placing obstacles in the way. The whole sacramental system becomes not merely sanctified but divinized with the redemptive and saving presence of the incarnate God.

The renewal in sacramental theology brings into clear relief the important truth that the incarnation is not an event like the birth of Caesar or the battle of Waterloo. They happened once and then became embalmed in the annals of the dead and buried past. But God's incarnation is perpetuated in the sacraments, providing them with their life-giving graces. Hence the recipient of any sacrament is meeting the God-man, Jesus Christ, as truly as Peter and Andrew met Him on the shore of the Sea of Galilee.

It is inspiring for the recipient to realize that in the sacraments he is meeting the selfsame Christ who died for him on Calvary's Cross and arose on Easter Sunday. His inspiration and joy would be greatly increased, however, if he would stop to realize that he is likewise encountering the invisible and transcendent God, of whom Jesus is the living and dynamic embodiment not only in

the Eucharist but also in all the other sacraments. Where Christ
is, there too is the Father.

This is the truth which Jesus taught by word, deed and especially
by His miracles. It is brought out beautifully and skillfully by
Christ in an incident related by the evangelist John (14:5-12).

"Lord," said the Apostle Thomas, "we do not know where thou
art going, and how can we know the way?"

"I am the way," replied Jesus, "and the truth, and the life. No
one comes to the Father but through me. If you had known me,
you would also have known the Father. And henceforth you do
know him, and you have seen him."

"Lord," said Philip eagerly, "show us the Father."

"Have I been so long a time with you," replied Jesus, "and you
have not known me? How canst thou say, 'Show us the Father'?
Dost thou not believe that I am in the Father and the Father in
me? The words that I speak to you I speak not on my own authority. But the Father dwelling in me, it is he who does the works.
Do you believe that I am in the Father and the Father in me?
Otherwise believe because of the works themselves."

Partakers of the Divine Nature

Thus Christ is perceived to be not merely a sign, symbol or image
of the transcendent God, but He bears God within Him and is
united indivisibly with Him. That is why students of sacramental
theology are not satisfied by calling Christ merely the Sacrament
of God but prefer the term "Primordial Sacrament" of God, to
bring out the unique and transcendent manner in which Jesus is
present and operative in all the sacraments. Thus the recipient of
the sacraments receives a grace which enables him to participate in
the divine nature which assimilates the soul to God and in a manner divinizes it.

This is the profound truth which St. Peter brings out in his
Second Epistle. "For indeed his divine power," says the Apostle,
"has granted us all things pertaining to life and piety through the
knowledge of him who has called us by his own glory and power
—through which he has granted us the very great and precious
promises, so that through them you may become *partakers of the*

divine nature" (1:4). This is the familiar intimacy with God which theologians call the divine indwelling, when the Triune God is present in the soul as the object of its love, contemplation and adoration.

Such indwelling of the Trinity constitutes the primary, paramount and most far-reaching effect of the state of grace. It leads man into the mysterious and hidden life of the Godhead, where he shares in the union of love in which that life consists. Divine grace forges a special link between the assimilated soul of the justified man and each person of the Trinity.

In his encyclical *Divinum Illud* Leo XIII pointed out that the union by indwelling differs only by reason of our earthly state from the union which the blessed enjoy in heaven. Enlarging upon this point in *Mystici Corporis,* Pius XII added that this vision of the blessed implies that they are the intimate witnesses of the processions of the three divine persons and thus enjoy a beatitude similar to that of the most holy and undivided Trinity. Thus does Christ as the Primordial Sacrament of God bring the recipient of all the sacraments into the most intimate participation in the life of the blessed Trinity. Only Christ could do this for, as St. Thomas points out, "the Word is not alone the unique revealer of the Godhead but indeed the *only* revealer consonant with the relations of the Trinity."

Christ: Sole Access to Salvation

Christ became the sacrament of God when He became man, and His life among men is the continuation and implementation of that sacrament. That Christ in His visible humanity is willed by God as the sole access to salvation is evidenced by the memorable words of St. Paul: "For there is only one mediator between God and man, the man Christ Jesus" (1 Tim. 2:5). Solely through the sacramentality of Christ can man achieve the intimate union with God and the beatific vision which constitute the enduring ecstasy of the blessed in heaven.

As the sacrament of God, Christ dispensed divine grace generously among the sick, the needy and the humble of heart who came to Him. Every encounter with Christ in a spirit of faith was an encounter with God, the source of all grace and holiness, and hence could be a sacrament. His invitation, "Come, follow me" (Mt. 4:19), to Andrew and Peter on the shore of the Sea of Galilee was clearly a sacramental grace.

His words, "Thy sins are forgiven" (Lk. 7:49), to the sinful woman who anointed His feet with her precious ointment, and His "Rise, take up thy pallet and walk" (Jn. 5:8), to the paralytic at the pool of Bethsaida were so many sacramental keys opening the treasury of heaven. After Peter had denied Christ the third time, the evangelist Luke tells us, "The Lord turned and looked upon Peter" and "Peter went out and wept bitterly" (22:61–62). Who can doubt that the glance of the Master, which brought in such abundance the grace of contrition, was indeed a sacrament?

When John the Baptist wanted to know the identity of the prophet and teacher about whom "the whole of Judea" was talking, he sent two of his disciples to find out. Approaching Jesus, they asked: "Art thou he who is to come, or shall we look for another?"

"Go and report to John," replied Jesus, "what you have heard and seen: the blind see, the lame walk, the lepers are cleansed, the deaf hear, the dead rise, the poor have the gospel preached to them" (Lk. 7:20–22). What were these actions, these gestures of Christ, but sacraments of healing? Encounters of these needy and afflicted people were encounters with Christ, the Primordial Sacrament of God.

It is through the cleansing, sanctifying and saving action of the sacraments that the compassionate Christ, who opened the flood gates of God's mercy, lives on in our midst, bringing to the people of every land and age the healing and redeeming power of His passion, death and resurrection.

The Incarnation: Sacrament of God's Love

The Incarnation itself might well seem to be the supreme and ultimate sacrament of God's love. What more could God do to show His love for man than to strip Himself of the glory of the Godhead and take upon Himself, as St. Paul says, "the form of a servant"? Yet He did more. He took upon Himself the sins of humanity and died for them upon the Cross. "Greater love than this," says the Evangelist John, "no one has, that one lay down his life for his friends" (15:13).

The work of redemption, however, was not yet complete. It finds its completion in the paschal mystery of the resurrection and ascension. That this was part of the original kerygma is clear from the words of the Apostle Paul: "I delivered to you what I also received, that Christ died for our sins according to the Scriptures, and that he was buried, *and* that he rose again the third day" (1 Cor. 15:3-4).

"It would do less than justice to the resurrection," Father O'Callaghan observes, "to regard it simply as a miracle, the supreme proof of Christ's divinity. That it certainly is, but it is a great deal more. It belongs in the very essence of the sacrifice of the passion in that it completes it as an efficacious sign. It is the victory over sin (*Christus victor mortis*), God's visible acceptance of the sacrifice of His Son, the full flowering of the hypostatic union; it consummates the alliance between God and men and establishes Christ as the *Kurios*, the glorified source of the new life now made available to the world."

Paschal Mystery: the Climax

From the moment of the incarnation Christ our high-priest offered all His work to His heavenly Father for the redemption and salvation of mankind. His priestly work was one of adoration and its climax was reached in the paschal mystery, when He passed over from mortal life through death to the resurrection and glory.

When Christ rose from the dead, He raised with Him all the members of the body of which He is the head, thus making the resurrection not merely a personal but a collective victory. This is the important truth which St. Paul expresses so beautifully: "But God, who is rich in mercy, by reason of his very great love wherewith he has loved us even when we were dead by reason of our sins, brought us to life together with Christ (by grace you have been saved), and raised us up together, and seated us together in heaven in Christ Jesus, that he might show in the ages to come the overflowing riches of his grace in kindness toward us in Christ Jesus" (Eph. 2:4–7).

Even though Christ has ascended into heaven and is no longer among us in bodily form, as the Primordial Sacrament He is still bestowing graces and blessings through the visible sacraments to perpetuate His sanctifying ministry and His saving presence. It was the realization of this great truth that prompted St. Leo (d. 461) to say: "That which formerly was visible in our Saviour has now passed into the mysteries," that is, the sacraments.

Even more vividly does St. Ambrose express the same vital truth: "You have shown thyself to me face to face, O Christ: I find Thee in the sacraments." Yes, Christ, the Primordial Sacrament of God, is present in all the sacraments. They are His personal acts and gestures, just as personal as when He cleansed the lepers, touched the eyes of the man born blind, and pardoned the thief on the cross. With the eyes of faith we can see Him acting in all the sacraments.

This is the truth which Pius XII stresses in *Mystici Corporis:* "It is Christ who baptizes . . . it is Christ who absolves . . . it is Christ who offers." With this vision in his mind surely every recipient will approach the sacraments with vastly greater devotion, reverence and love. Then he will have not only a theoretical but also an experiential knowledge of what Jesus meant when He said: "If anyone love me . . . my Father will love him, and will come to him and make our abode with him" (Jn. 14:23).

VII.

THE CHURCH:
THE SACRAMENT OF CHRIST

As Christ in His visible humanity was the sacrament of God, so the Church in all its visibility and human imperfections is the sacrament of Christ. While there is no hypostatic union between Christ and the Church, as there is between the humanity and the divinity of Christ, there is a mystical union so intimate and so real that the Church can properly be called, in the famous words of the Apostle Paul, "the body of Christ" (1 Cor. 12:27). The Church is the prolongation of the incarnation in time and space and the perpetuation of the redemptive activity of Christ.

During His earthly ministry Jesus was the visible and effective symbol of the saving mercy, compassion and love of God. In a similar manner the Church is the visible and effective sign or sacrament of the redemption communicated to men. As the Saviour, who gave His life on Calvary's Cross for us, was the visible image of the invisible God, so too is the Church the visible image of the invisible Christ. "Just as we cannot bypass the Christ," Father Palmer says, "in our encounter with God, so too we cannot bypass the Church in our encounter with Christ."

While the concept of the Church as the sacrament of Christ is not completely new, it is only in recent years that it has been stressed. This has been due largely to the pioneering work of the German theologians Karl Rahner and Otto Semmelroth and the Dutch theologian Edward Schillebeeckx. Back of the notion is the traditional doctrine that in the Church the incarnation of Christ and His redeeming mission are mysteriously prolonged. In the life and work of the Church Christ's offer of friendship is both revealed and actualized.

Just as Israel was a sacrament of the Old Law, symbolizing God's presence among the chosen people, so the Church is a basic sacrament of the New Law, symbolizing and effectuating His presence among its members. The presence of Christ in the Church and His identity with it was a favorite theme of St. Paul and stems apparently from his extraordinary conversion. While on his way to Damascus to persecute Christians, he was suddenly stricken to the ground and blinded by a light from heaven.

"Saul, Saul," he heard a voice saying, "why dost thou persecute me?"

"Who art thou, Lord?" he asked.

"I am Jesus," came the reply, "whom thou art persecuting" (Acts 9:4–5).

From a rabid persecutor of the Church Saul was transformed into the ardent and intrepid Apostle Paul, who was destined to proclaim the Gospel of Christ to the Gentiles. The Apostle could never forget that Christ did not ask why he was persecuting Christians but "Why dost thou persecute *me?*" This identification of Christ with His Church and its members penetrated so deeply into the consciousness of Paul that he was forever afterwards struggling to express it.

He repeatedly refers to the Church as the body of Christ. "We being many are one body in Christ, and all members one of another" (Rom. 12:5). "He is the head of His body, the Church," while we "are together the body of Christ and severally His members" (1 Cor. 12:27). "I rejoice now in the sufferings I bear for your sake; and what is lacking of the sufferings of Christ I fill up in my flesh for his body which is the Church" (Col. 1:24).

The Church: Body of Christ

Other writers and Fathers of the early Church liked to dwell upon the Church as the body of Christ, particularly St. Irenaeus, Tertullian, St. Ambrose, St. John Chrysostom and, above all, St. Augustine. "Christ's body," says St. Augustine, "is the Church, not this Church or that Church, but the Church throughout the world. . . . The members of Christ are bound together by the union of charity, and by that self-same charity they are united to their head, who is Christ Jesus . . . Wishest thou to live of Christ's spirit? Then be in Christ's body."

With the Apostles gathered about Him at the Last Supper, Jesus reveals to them how closely the members of His Church must be united to Him, achieving a living organic unity. "I am the vine," He says, "you are the branches. He who abides in me, and I in him, he bears much fruit; for without me you can do nothing" (Jn. 15:5).

Later on that evening Jesus raised His eyes to heaven and uttered His memorable prayer for unity. "Holy Father," He prayed, "keep in thy name those whom thou hast given me, that they may be one even as we are" (Jn. 17:11). No more intimate union of distinct persons than that of the Father and the Son in the Holy Trinity can be conceived. Yet it is not only for the unity of the Apostles that Jesus prays but for "those also who through their word are to believe in me, that they all may be one, even as thou, Father, in me and I in thee; that they also may be *one in us,* that the world may believe that thou hast sent me" (Jn. 17:20–21).

Seeking to assure the Apostles of His abiding presence and even identity with them in their ministry of preaching, Jesus says: "He who hears you, hears me, and he who rejects you, rejects me; and he who rejects me, rejects him who sent me" (Lk. 10:16). The climax of such assurance that Jesus would abide with the members of His Church would seem to be reached after the resurrection, when He met with the Apostles for the last time on a mountain in Galilee.

The evangelist Matthew ends his Gospel with those solemn words which bring it to such a majestic climax: "Go, therefore," says Jesus, "and make disciples of all nations, baptizing them in the name of the Father, and of the Son, and of the Holy Spirit, teaching them to observe all that I have commanded you; and behold, I am with you all days, even unto the consummation of the world" (28:19–20).

The Flowering of Two Doctrines

We have presented the teaching of Christ, St. Paul and the Fathers of the Church concerning the union of Christ with His Church, of which He is the head and we are the members. Hence the Church is called the Mystical Body of Christ. What is the relevance of this to our theme—the Church as the sacrament of Christ? This latter concept is the beautiful flowering of the doctrines of the indwelling of Christ in His Church and of the mediatorship of Christ through His Church as set forth in the passages of Scripture just quoted and in the two encyclicals of Pius XII: *Mystici Corporis* issued in June, 1943, and *Mediator Dei* issued in November, 1947.

In the first encyclical Pius XII points out that the Church is the body of Christ not only because He is the head but also because "He so sustains the Church, and so in a certain sense lives in the Church, that it is, as it were, another Christ." Developing this truth, the pontiff states that our "Saviour shares his most personal prerogatives with the Church in such a way that she may portray in her whole life, both external and internal, a most faithful *image* of Christ."

Here is the sacramental concept of the Church as an effective sign or image of Christ, communicating His divine life and grace to the souls of its members. Christ does not merely live in a house as a tenant in an apartment building, who retains his resources and shares none with the others. Christ living in the Church communicates His saving presence and His divine riches to all who dwell therein. It is this sharing action of Christ within the Church that makes the Church in a real and profound sense the basic sacrament of Christ.

While nothing can be added to the perfect worship which Christ our High Priest rendered to the Father, we must be drawn into that worship if we are to share the divine life of grace. Hence the eternal act of homage, offered by Christ in the paschal mystery of His death, resurrection and ascension, is made present for us in the Church. "Since the resurrection," says the *Catholic Encyclopedia for School and Home,* "true Christian worship of Christ consists in the sacramentalizing of the heavenly worship that Christ is forever offering at the Father's right hand. This sacramental worship is made ours when Christ acts in and with His Church. As He worshipped the Father while on earth and thus saved men, so He now offers this same worship in His Mystical Body, the Church."

Some time ago a section of New York City was paralyzed by an electrical power failure in one of the city power plants. The newspapers presented a vivid picture of the resulting inconvenience and chaos. For thirteen hours the residents were without light; their refrigerators failed to work. Men shaving with electric shavers found them coming to a dead stop. Customers in supermarkets lined up in long rows before dead cash registers while clerks tallied up their purchases with pencil and paper.

Most seriously affected were the patients in the dozen hospitals in that area. Surgical operations were suddenly and unexpectedly halted. An iron-lung patient was kept alive by a respirator operated by a pair of nurses. Using portable incubators, doctors and nurses rushed premature infants some 70 blocks to a downtown hospital. This disruption of the normal life of the residents of that section illustrates what would happen on the spiritual plane if the divine power and energy of Christ operating within the Church should suddenly cease.

The Church: Continuation of Christ

In the divine plan salvation comes to me through Christ operating within the Church which He established for their sanctification and salvation. This implies union with Christ and the Church. Before coming to our Creator we must come to Christ, and before coming to our Saviour we must come to the Church, which is Christ continued and made visible in time.

In his stimulating book *Catholicism,* rich in fresh insights, Henri de Lubac stresses this point. "Grace does not set up," he says, "a purely individual relationship between the soul and God or Christ; rather, each one receives grace in the measure in which he is joined socially to that unique organism in which there flows its life-giving stream. . . . All the sacraments are essentially sacraments in the Church; in her alone they produce their full effect, for in her alone, the society of the Spirit, is there, normally speaking, a sharing in the gift of the Spirit."

It is interesting to note that de Lubac considers the concept of salvation, in which the Christian is united to God and to Christ in the Church, through his membership in the churchly community, is the "constant teaching of the Church" though he acknowledges that "in practice it is too little known." During Christ's earthly ministry the actions of God become visible in and through the humanity of our divine Redeemer. The actions of the glorified Christ in heaven now become visible in and through His body, the Church, thus making the latter the living sacrament of Christ.

Salvation: No Solitary Affair

In the divine plan salvation is not merely a solitary affair. It has marked social and community implications. This is evident from salvation history as related in the Bible. Israel was God's Chosen People, to whom He sent first the prophets and lastly His own beloved Son. They were the objects of His solicitude and predilection, and upon them He lavished innumerable blessings and favors.

The Hebrew people were to achieve their salvation through union with Yahweh in the synagogue and in the temple with its Holy of Holies, sacrifices, Torah, Talmud, Ark of the Covenant and its holy prophets and rabbis. So too the people of the New Covenant are to find their salvation in union with Christ in the Church with its holy Scriptures, liturgy and sacraments.

Israel was the prototype of the Church, which is being described with increasing frequency as the People of God. The term emphasizes the community aspect of the Primordial Sacrament established by Christ to perpetuate His redemptive mission among men and to communicate to them the fruits of the paschal mystery of His passion, death, resurrection and ascension. Hence salvation is normally achieved through membership in the churchly community in which Christ lives, acts and communicates with His people. Just as the Hebrew people would have been appalled at the thought of achieving salvation apart from the synagogue, so Christians, worthy of the name, would be horrified at the thought of attaining eternal union with God apart from the Church of which Christ is the head and the Holy Spirit is the soul. St. Cyprian (d. 258) reflected the faith of the early Church when he said: "No one can have God for Father who does not have the Church for Mother."

The Church: Family of God

The Church is not merely the people of God: it is also the "family of God," with all the endearing connotations of that heart-warming phrase. In that spacious household of the faith, whose dimensions are vaster than those of the universe, man finds not only his father and mother but also his brothers and sisters, who through the centuries were nourished by the seven sacraments and especially by the heavenly manna of the holy Eucharist. The family of God is a mysterious extension of the blessed Trinity in time and space.

In the mighty family of God we are united with all the saints, sages and martyrs of the race. "We have at our disposal," observes Paul Claudel, "for loving, understanding and serving God not only our own powers but everything from the Blessed Virgin in the summit of heaven down to the poor African leper who, bell in hand, whispers the responses of Mass through a mouth half eaten away. The whole of creation, visible and invisible, all history, all the past, the present and the future, all the treasure of the saints— all that is at our disposal as an extension of ourselves, a mighty instrument."

The family of God banishes our sense of loneliness in a cosmos so stupendous as to dwarf us at every turn. It ministers to our deepest immemorial yearnings and provides us with the means of fulfilling them. The deepest of these yearnings is for union with the God who brought us into being. After many years of searching for happiness in areas where it can never be found, St. Augustine cried out: "Our hearts have been made for Thee, O God, and they shall never rest until they rest in Thee." Those words find an answering echo in every human heart.

The great family of God, which we call the Church, provides both the light and the strength to enable us to attain our eternal destiny in a union with the Triune God of such intimacy that it approximates the union of the three Persons—Father, Son and Holy Spirit. In the mysterious unity of the great family of God, where "many are one," we have a foretaste of that unique and transcendental unity which we all shall experience when we are brought together into the life of the Most Holy Trinity. Thus does the Church in its community aspect as "the people of God" and "the family of God" serve as an effective sign or sacrament of Christ, whom it not only symbolizes but with whom it also enables us to achieve an abiding union.

The Climax of Christ's Redemptive Mission

Through the Church as the primordial sacrament, Christ perpetuates in a mysterious manner His redemptive mission which reached its crowning climax in His death on Calvary's Cross. From His passion and death stem all the graces which flow through the Church into its sevenfold sacramental outlets. This is the point which the Apostle Paul stresses when he writes to the Romans: "Do you not know that all we who have been baptized into Christ Jesus have been baptized into his death" (6:3). Thus does the Apostle connect the sacraments with Christ's passion and especially His death as the sources of their efficacy.

From the Apostolic era Christian tradition has held in special reverence the moment when the centurion with his lance pierced the side of the crucified Christ and saw blood and water issue from it. The Fathers and St. Thomas have regarded that stream as the symbol of the sacraments and through these as the sign of the Church, the new Eve created from the side of the new Adam as he slept.

Through the reception of the sacraments members of the Church are brought into communication with the passion of Christ and receive its effects. Thus the sacramental sign always recalls Christ's saving death and the sacraments cause us to enter into the paschal mystery of His death, resurrection and ascension to His Father. "Christ died," said St. Augustine, "that the Church might be born. His side was pierced with a lance in order that there might flow forth the sacraments from which the Church was formed." The water and wine have been construed by the Fathers and Doctors of the Church as the symbols of the two principal sacraments—baptism and the Eucharist.

From the day on which the Church issued from the pierced side of Christ, it has been the earthly sign of the triumphant redeeming grace of Christ and it shall so remain until the last soul is gathered unto the eternal hills. It shall remain, however, not merely as a sign but as an effective one, producing and communicating to its members the redeeming grace which it so wondrously symbolizes. In so doing, the Church stands out conspicuously, in the words of the First Vatican Council, as "the sign raised up among the nations"—the primary sacrament of Christ.

Christ is present in the Church as the primeval sacrament and acts in all the subsidiary sacraments which convey His redeeming grace to man. Because of his intention to do what the Church does, the minister becomes the agent through whom Christ acts. In the last analysis it is not Peter or Paul who baptizes, but Christ. In pouring the water, their hands become the hands of Christ and in speaking the words their voices but echo the voice of Christ. Hence it is that St. Augustine was able to point out that neither sin nor even heresy on the part of the minister impedes the flow of sacramental grace.

"Those who were baptized by John the Baptist," he says, "were given baptism again. Now Jesus Himself did not baptize, but His disciples did, and Judas was still among them. How can it be that those who were baptized by John had to be baptized again, and not those baptized by Judas? Certainly . . . those whom John baptized were baptized by John: those whom Judas baptized were baptized by Christ." Though the ministers of the sacraments are many, there is but one High Priest, Jesus Christ, acting through them in the Church.

The Church: Extension of Christ's Humanity

As the sacramental extension of the sacred humanity of Jesus, the Church is a divine organism in which its members are nourished with divine life. By baptism we are "grafted" into Christ's body, as St. Paul tells us in the Epistle to the Romans (11:24). The aptness of the Pauline image of grafting becomes evident when we scrutinize a bit more closely what this operation involves.

When a twig from an elm tree, for example, is grafted onto an oak tree, the twig retains the characteristics of an elm tree but lives by the vital nourishment supplied by the host—the oak tree. In similar fashion, when we are grafted by baptism into the body of Christ, we retain the characteristics of a human being, but we are nourished with the supernatural and divine life of our host—the body of Christ. Streaming through that body are all the sacramental graces which ultimately reach the recipients of the various subsidiary sacraments. Here again we see how apt are the terms we apply to the Church as both the Mystical Body and the primary sacrament of Christ.

That the Church serves as the essential medium and basic sacrament for the dispensing of the graces of the crucified Christ is brought out beautifully by Pius XII in *Mystici Corporis:* "As He hung upon the Cross, Christ Jesus not only avenged the justice of the eternal Father that had been flouted, but He also won for us, His brothers, an unending flow of graces. It was possible for Him personally, immediately to impart these graces to men; but He wished to do so only through a visible Church that would be formed by the union of men, and thus through that Church every man would perform a work of collaboration with Him in dispensing the graces of redemption. The Word of God willed to make use of our nature, when in excruciating agony He would redeem mankind; in much the same way throughout the centuries He makes use of the Church that the work begun might endure."

Christ's ministry on earth was manifold: He healed the sick, cleansed the leper, restored sight to the blind, hearing to the deaf and speech to the dumb. He exorcised those possessed by evil spirits, He forgave sinners, He preached the Gospel, He offered homage to the heavenly Father and restored vigor of limb to the paralytic. As the primary sacrament of Christ, the Church continues this varied ministry through the sacraments.

The Church: Perpetuation of Christ's Ministry

A perpetuation of His sanctifying epiphany among men, the sacraments point to the Christ of yesterday, the Christ of today and the Christ who remains with the people of God forever. As our High Priest, Jesus is operative in our midst today in a manner more wonderful and effective than when He walked with His disciples along the shores of the Sea of Galilee and over the dusty roads of Judea and Samaria.

Then His ministry reached a few thousand. Now through the sacraments He reaches untold millions. Then the 12 Apostles and the 72 disciples walked *with* Christ. Now countless millions live *in* His body, the Church. In a manner more wonderful than the

Apostles could ever have imagined, Christ is fulfilling the promise made to them when He commissioned them to go, baptize and teach, and assured them that He would be *with* them "all days, even unto the consummation of the world" (Mt. 28:19–20). Through the sacraments we are now not only *with* Him but actually live *in* Him.

In treating of Christ as the Primordial Sacrament of God and the Church as the primary sacrament of Christ, it is obvious, of course, that we have been using the word "sacrament" in a more general and extensive sense than when it is used in connection with the seven sacraments. The very concept of Christ and of the Church as sacraments, brought to the fore by the theological renewal, exalts the entire sacramental system by emphasizing both the presence and the activity of Christ and the Church in each of the seven sacraments.

It helps the recipient to realize more clearly and vividly than ever before that the sacraments are personal encounters with God, Jesus Christ and the Holy Spirit as well as with the Church. In each sacrament he is thus enabled, with the eyes of faith, to perceive Christ communicating His sanctifying grace and redeeming love to his soul, in which the three persons of the blessed Trinity are taking up their abode. By emphasizing the important truth that sacraments are personal encounters with the triune God, the theological renewal makes the recipients more keenly conscious that they are called upon to respond actively to God's offer of love and grace and not be merely passive spectators.

Man Speaks, God Replies

As in all true dialogues there is conversation by both parties, so in the sacraments, God speaks and man replies. While the grace received through the sacraments is far greater than that which the recipient could merit by his acts of devotion, the sacramental grace is proportioned to the depth and fervor of the faith, hope, love and devotion of the recipient.

"Without our response to God in sacramental encounters," according to the *Catholic Encyclopedia for School and Home*, "there can be no union with God, no fruitful sacramental experience. Of all the sacraments, therefore, it must be said that they are signs of faith, the faith of the Church and of the individual involved. When the latter is lacking, one fails to make the sign to be for him what it is as such, a sign of Christian worship. True faith includes the dedication to a fuller commitment to Christ. At each meeting with Christ sacramentally we renew our loyalty to His New Covenant; we profess our willingness to live more earnestly our vocation as members of the people of God, and in proportion to the sincerity of this profession we are drawn into closer unity with God through grace."

Such then is the renewal of sacramental theology which has been brought about by the prolonged studies and profound meditation of Biblical scholars and theologians under the influence of the Holy Spirit and the new religious climate which the ecumenical movement has helped to create. The balance between sign and causality, upset at least in practice for more than four centuries, has been happily and providentially restored.

VIII.

THE BIBLICAL REVIVAL

THE liturgical renewal has sparked revivals in many fields and has, in turn, been enriched by them. A notable instance of this is the Biblical revival which has already produced notable results and in consequence has brought into being a new branch of sacred science called Biblical theology. What were the factors which have brought about the modern Biblical renaissance, generally acclaimed as the most fruitful Scriptural development in the entire history of the Church?

There were several factors. The first was doubtless the cruel shattering of the widespread illusion, that science and technology could build a safe, efficient and prosperous civilization, brought about by the holocaust of World War II. Instead of rendering human progress certain and inevitable, they presented us with new and fearful instruments for the obliteration of the human race from the face of the earch.

With the hydrogen bomb hanging like the sword of Damocles over their heads, men turned desperately to God and religion to save them from their own destructive ferocity. With new and feverish interest they opened their Bibles to learn about God's plan of salvation and to secure the spiritual nourishment they so sorely needed. This demanded that they study the Bible with new diligence and care in order properly to understand its momentous and salutary truths. This, in turn, required Scriptural scholars to present these truths in popular language.

A second factor was the astonishing discovery of the Dead Sea Scrolls, more properly called the Qumran Manuscripts. They are a collection of 100 Biblical manuscripts, mostly in Hebrew, and other literary fragments which were found between 1947 and 1952 in six caves in the Desert of Juda west of the Dead Sea.

Among the incredible treasures were a complete Hebrew text of Isaia dating from the second century B.C., other Old Testament texts including the deuterocanonical Tobia, collections of messianic texts, a commentary on the Book of Habbacuc, and apocalyptic writings. The enormous significance of these findings becomes evident when one learns that, until their discovery, the oldest known Hebrew manuscripts were from the tenth century A.D.

The discovery of these Biblical manuscripts thus takes us back more than a thousand years and discloses to us the nature of the Old Testament before and at the time of Christ. The Qumran Manuscripts are thought to have belonged to the Essenes and are considered important sources of information about Hebrew literature, Jewish history during the period between the Old and New Testaments, and the history of the Septuagint of the Old Testament.

Joseph A. Fitzmyer, S.J., of the American School of Oriental Research at Jerusalem, has remarked that "It is difficult to exaggerate the importance of the Dead Sea Scrolls for the study of the New Testament and of Christian origins. When we consider only that previous to their discovery no documents, practically speaking, from Palestine of the first century B.C. or A.D.—aside from a few funerary inscriptions—were extant, the value of these texts becomes apparent. We have now in the Dead Sea Scrolls texts which reveal to us the language spoken at the time of Christ and the language used in literary writings."

The third factor contributing to the present Biblical revival was the wealth of Scriptural data accumulated by the end of World War II. Through the application of critical and historical methods to the study of the Bible, giant strides had been taken in determining the concrete facts concerning literary origins, oriental idioms, the progress of Old Testament revelation and the ethnic and political environment of the Hebrews. The study of monuments and the excavation of ancient sites brought new light from the East. Comparative philology and the scientific study of languages yielded new and important information.

Rationalists had long been using the new findings for their own purposes. It was imperative for Catholic scholars to use the new methods and the new data for the perfection of their exegesis. Since the turn of the century Protestant scholars had been doing this and were in consequence considerably ahead of us. Fearful of the modernist heresy which affected some Scriptural scholars such as Alfred Loisy, Rome had silenced a number of Catholics, including our most eminent Biblicist, Père M. J. Lagrange, O.P., founder of the famous Ecole Biblique in Jerusalem.

The Magna Carta of Biblical Renewal

This period of enforced silence, which lasted about forty years, was ended on September 30, 1943, when Pius XII issued the encyclical *Divino Afflante Spiritu,* which has become the Magna Carta of our modern Biblical renaissance. This is the fourth and doubtless the most important factor contributing to that revival. The encyclical not only shattered the shackles of silence but also encouraged and even urged Catholic scholars to use the new methods of scientific research to understand more clearly the revealed word of God.

This was the signal for which Catholic exegetes had long been waiting. With boundless zeal and enthusiasm they plunged in, and their work has enormously increased our understanding of the Bible. Typical of the results of such research is the Jerusalem Bible, edited by the Dominicans in Jerusalem and enriched with historical and doctrinal notes. It is regarded by many Biblicists as without a peer in the world today. Other examples of Catholic research are the Echter Bible and the Bonner Bible in Germany, and the Confraternity Old Testament in the U.S. Typical of the research of Protestant scholars in the English-speaking world is the excellent Revised Standard Version.

Another fruit of Scriptural research, as previously indicated, is the birth of the discipline of Biblical theology. This is the study of divine truth as expressed in Scripture, analyzed and systematized according to Biblical categories. Take, for example, the concept of faith. Instead of defining it in an abstract manner after studying the concept in scholastic philosophy and theology as the speculative theologian does, the Biblical theologian turns to the Bible and examines the concepts of faith as found in all its books.

He then assembles these concepts with all their various shadings and nuances and thus penetrates to the heart of this idea as revealed in the words of Holy Writ mirroring the thought of God Himself. This procedure thus respects the primacy of the operation of the Holy Spirit in revelation and the unique pre-eminence of holy Scripture as the record of that operation.

The Peerless Norm of Divine Truth

Despite the existence of a divine and apostolic tradition, Holy Writ remains an excellent and incomparable source and a peerless norm for the ascertainment of divine truth. Consequently, as Karl Rahner says, "when dogmatic theology as a whole listens to God's written word in and with the authoritative Church, which itself is bound to listen attentively to Scripture, something totally unique occurs. Here and here alone, dogmatic theology is directed and does not direct, listens without really passing judgment, as it does in its other historical and speculative functions. Though it is a beginning, the pure beginning of the kerygma of the faith which is ever-present in Scripture always remains something greater and more comprehensive, a principle constantly giving rise to new development which it pervades and governs. Biblical theology consists in a return to this principle, not in the collection of proof-texts."

Especially significant is the contribution of history, linguistics and archeology to the Biblical renaissance in providing the new approach to the sacred text by the analysis of the literary form or genre involved. This does not affect in the slightest way the inspired character of the sacred document. Since any mention of the "literary form" of a sacred document disturbs many people including some clerics, and leads them to suspect that this implies a denial of its inspired character, it is well to quote Pope Pius XII on this point.

In *Divino Afflante Spiritu,* Pope Pius XII says: "But frequently the literal sense is not so obvious in the words and writings of ancient oriental authors as it is with the writers of today. What they intended to signify by their words is not determined only by the laws of grammar and philology or merely by the context. It is absolutely necessary for the interpreter to go back in spirit to those remote centuries of the East, and make proper use of aids afforded by history, archeology, ethnology and other sciences in order to discover what literary forms the writers of that early age intended to use and did in fact employ; for to express what they had in mind, the ancients of the East did not always use the same forms and expressions that we use today. They used those that were current among the people of their own time and place. What these were, the exegete cannot determine *a priori,* but only from the careful study of ancient oriental literature."

Referring to the fruitfulness of such study, the pope continues: "This study has been pursued during the past few decades with greater care and industry than formerly, and has made us better acquainted with the literary forms used in those ancient times, whether in poetical descriptions or in formulation of rules and laws of conduct, or in the narration of historical facts and events. It has now clearly demonstrated the unique pre-eminence among all the ancient nations of the East, which the people of Israel enjoyed in historical writing, both in regard to the antiquity of the events recorded and to the accuracy with which they are related. A circumstance which is, of course, explained by the *charism* of divine inspiration, and by the special religious purpose of Biblical history."

Warning readers not to be surprised if they find in the Bible certain forms of narrative not in use by historians today, the pope says: "At the same time no one who has a just conception of Biblical inspiration will be surprised to find that the sacred writers, like the other ancients, employ certain arts of exposition and narrative, certain idioms especially characteristic of the Semitic languages (known as approximations) and certain hyperbolical and even paradoxical expressions designed for the sake of emphasis. The sacred books need not exclude any of the forms of expression which were commonly used in human speech by the ancient peoples, especially of the East, to convey their meaning so long as they are in no way incompatible with God's sanctity and God's truth."

New Freedom for Catholic Scholars

Here the pope makes it clear that any literary form may be found in the Bible, provided it does not contradict the truth or the holiness of God. To get across their messages to the people of their day the sacred writers used a great variety of literary forms: poetry, canti-

cles, fable, saga and didactic fiction are but a few of the many gen-
res. Thus the Book of Jona, modern exegetes are agreed, is an
excellent example of didactic fiction. To a people steeped in the idea
of particularism it gets across its message that the love and mercy
of God transcend the limits of tribe or race and extend to all men,
and it does this in a delightful, pungent and arresting manner.

To appreciate the freedom of Catholic scholars to use the new
methods of historical, linguistic, archeological research and the encouragement given to them to do so, one should read the *Divino
Afflante Spiritu* in its entirety. This great encyclical has virtually
revolutionized the techniques of Catholic research and has served as
a powerful catalyst in bringing about the present Biblical renewal.

The fifth factor contributing to this revival is the growth of the
ecumenical movement which was underway long before the Second
Council. This heightened the consciousness of all Biblical scholars
that they have a common problem: the attainment of a better understanding of the divine truths recorded in Holy Writ. There is no
room for sectarianism here. A discovery by one enriches all. The
pursuit of truth is the tie which binds all Scriptural scholars in a
common loyalty and dedication.

This new spirit of understanding, warmth and friendship has
opened doors long closed and has leveled ancient barriers which
precluded cooperative action. Now Biblical scholars, Protestant,
Catholic and Jewish, are working shoulder to shoulder in the excit-
ing enterprise of ferreting out the real meaning of every verse of the
Old and New Testaments.

A common Bible for all Christians is the goal toward which many
scholars are working. The Fathers at the fourth session of Vatican
Council II have spoken encouragingly and hopefully of such a
project. Indeed a significant step in that direction was taken in 1965
with the publication of a Catholic edition of the Protestant Revised
Standard Version of the New Testament.

Embodying a special introduction and explanatory notes, the
edition received the *imprimatur* of Archbishop J. Gray of St. Andrew's and Edinburgh, Scotland, and the approval of the Congregation of the Holy Office. Catholic scholars who worked on the edition
were members of a committee established for the purpose by the
bishops of England, Scotland and Wales. Giving complete coopera-

tion for the joint publication effort was the National Council of the Churches of Christ in the U.S., the sponsor and copyright holder of the Revised Standard Version.

Such are the highlights of the Biblical renaissance which has already profoundly influenced the life, thought and action of the Church. It has stimulated the catechetical revival, provided a Scriptural basis for the liturgical movement, heightened the ecumenical spirit and brought Catholic and non-Catholic Biblical scholars to join in cooperative undertakings. It is rich in the promise of bridging the differences which have so long separated Christians and may prove to be one of the chief means designated by divine Providence to achieve the long-cherished dream of Christian unity.

IX.

THE ECUMENICAL MOVEMENT

THE word "ecumenism" is derived from a Greek term meaning world-wide. Ecumenism is a movement which seeks to establish unity among all persons and Churches calling themselves Christian. Only Catholics are united in a single Church having unity of faith, worship, discipline and government. While sharing many points of belief and practice with Catholics, the Orthodox belong to autonomous Churches. Protestants belong to a great number of denominations—of which there are some 250 in the U.S. alone—with basic differences in belief, worship, discipline and government.

The modern ecumenical movement is generally regarded as having its beginning at the meeting of the World Missionary Conference in Edinburgh in 1910. For almost fifty years it developed outside the mainstream of Catholic interest. The Catholic movement began in 1959, when Pope John XXIII announced that one of the objectives of the Second Vatican Council would be the exploration of ways and means of promoting unity among all persons professing faith.

For this purpose he established the Vatican Secretariat for Promoting Christian Unity which extended cordial invitations to Protestant and Eastern Orthodox Churches to send observers. Many did so, with the result that the ecumenical movement gained vastly greater vigor and dynamism. Pope Paul VI has continued the policy of his predecessor, and the Second Vatican Council has focused worldwide attention upon the Church's efforts to promote Christian unity. These were climaxed by the enactment of the *Decree on Ecumenism*.

The Scriptural basis of the ecumenical movement is found chiefly in the teachings of Christ and the Apostle Paul. In His parables Our

Lord often spoke of the Kingdom of heaven or of God, which was always described as one society. It was an undivided kingdom, otherwise it would come to ruin (Mt. 12:25). This kingdom was His Church not Churches. "And I say to thee, thou art Peter, and upon this rock I will build my Church, and the gates of hell shall not prevail against it" (Mt. 16:18).

There is but one Shepherd, Jesus insists, and one flock. "I am the good shepherd," He says, "and I know mine and mine know me, even as the Father knows me and I know the Father; and I lay down my life for my sheep. And other sheep I have that are not of this fold. Them also I must bring, and they shall hear my voice, and there shall be one fold and one shepherd" (Jn. 10:14-16).

Jesus likens Himself to the vine and His disciples to the branches and stresses the unity of both: "I am the true vine . . . Abide in me, and I in you. As the branch cannot bear fruit of itself unless it remain on the vine, so neither can you unless you abide in me. I am the vine, you are the branches. He who abides in me, and I in him, he bears much fruit; for without me you can do nothing. If anyone does not abide in me, he shall be cast outside as the branch and wither; and they shall gather them up and cast them into the fire, and they shall burn" (Jn. 15:1-6).

Christ's Most Impressive Utterance

Most impressive and memorable of all of Christ's utterances on this subject is His prayer at the Last Supper for the unity of all His followers. "Holy Father," Jesus prays, "keep in thy name those whom thou hast given me, that they may be one even as we are. . . . Yet not for these [His disciples] only do I pray, but for those also who through their word are to believe in me, that all may be one, even as thou, Father, in me and I in thee; that they also may be one in us, that the world may believe that thou hast sent me" (Jn. 17:11-22).

The Apostle Paul solemnly warns the Corinthians against violating the unity upon which Christ had so strongly insisted. "Now I beseech you, brethren," he says, "by the name of our Lord Jesus Christ, that you all say the same thing; and that there be no dissensions among you, but that you be perfectly united in one mind and in one judgment" (1 Cor. 1:10).

Stressing the necessity of holding fast to the Gospel of Christ and thus preserving unity of faith, the Apostle writes to the Galatians: "I marvel that you are so quickly deserting him who called you to the grace of Christ, changing to another Gospel; which is not another Gospel, except in this respect that there are some who trouble you, and wish to pervert the Gospel of Christ. But even if we or an angel from heaven should preach a Gospel to you other than that which we have preached to you, let him be anathema!" (Gal. 1:6–8).

Recurring to this same theme later on in his letter, the Apostle says: "For you are all the children of God through faith in Christ Jesus. For all you who have been baptized into Christ, have put on Christ. There is neither Jew nor Greek; there is neither slave nor freeman; there is neither male nor female. For you are all one in Christ Jesus" (Gal. 3:26–28).

"One Lord, One Faith"

From his prison in Rome, St. Paul writes to the Ephesians: "I, therefore, the prisoner in the Lord, exhort you to walk in a manner worthy of the calling with which you were called, with all humanity and meekness, with patience, bearing with one another in love, careful to preserve the unity of the Spirit in the bond of peace: one body and one Spirit, even as you were called in one hope of your calling; one Lord, one faith, one baptism; one God and Father of all, who is above all, and throughout all, and in us all" (4:1–6).

The stern insistence by Christ and the Apostles, especially St. Paul, upon absolute unity in faith and worship made an indelible impression upon the early Christians, which is mirrored in the writings of the Fathers and Doctors of the Church. Writing in the third century, Tertullian thus testifies to this unity: "We are a society with a common religious feeling, unity of discipline, and a common bond of hope."

Outstanding among the early Fathers in his repeated stress upon unity is St. Cyprian, Bishop of Carthage, who lived in the third century. "God is one," he writes, "and Christ is one, His Church is one, His see is one, founded by the voice of the Lord on Peter. No other altar can be set up, no other priesthood instituted apart from that one altar and that one priesthood. Whoso gathers elsewhere, scatters." Memorable too are his oft-quoted words: "He cannot have God for his Father who has not the Church for his mother."

Writing in the fourth century, St. Hilary of Poitiers bears witness to the unity of the Church: "Although there is one Church throughout the world, still each city has its own Church. The Church is one in all these." In the following century St. Augustine, Bishop of Hippo, testifies to the unity of Christians: "All mankind is in Christ one man, and the unity of Christians is one Man."

Such then are the teachings of holy Scripture and of the Fathers and Doctors of the Church upon the unity of faith and worship which Christ wanted to characterize all His followers. Climaxing this demand for unity was His prayer at the Last Supper. The memory of those words, "that all may be one, even as thou, Father, in me and I in thee," haunts Christians today and fills them with a sense of guilt as they gaze upon their many divisions.

New Dimensions

This has led to the ecumenical movement which has reached new dimensions today. Among its fruits are the World Council of Churches and the Second Vatican Council. The latter produced the important *Decree on Ecumenism*. Promulgated by Pope Paul VI on November 21, 1964, the decree provides authoritative guidance for Catholic participants in the movement for Christian unity. Let us consider some of the highlights of this important document.

It declares that the restoration of unity among all Christians is one of the chief concerns of the Council since the present division contradicts the will of Christ, scandalizes the world and impairs the effectiveness of the Church's witness to the world. Praising the efforts of Protestants toward unity, the Council encourages Catholics to take an active part in this world-wide movement. It points out that Christian renewal must begin with the individual; each one must deepen his own interior life and put into practice Christ's law of love.

The Council instructs Catholics to acknowledge and esteem the Christian endowments from our common heritage, which are to be found among our separated brethren. We must recognize the riches of Christ and the holiness in the lives of other Christians, which have prompted some of them to bear witness to Christ even to the shedding of their blood. "Whatever is truly Christian," says the Council, "is never contrary to what genuinely belongs to the faith; indeed it can always bring a more perfect realization of the very mystery of Christ and the Church" (# 4).

Continual Reformation

The Church is summoned to a continual reformation, of which she has need in so far as she is an institution of men. Such renewal has notable ecumenical significance. Indeed it is already manifesting itself in the biblical and liturgical movements, the preaching of the word of God and catechetics, the apostolate of the laity, new forms of religious life, a deeper spirituality of married life and the Church's social teachings and activity.

Quoting the words of the evangelist John that all men have sinned, the Council points out that this holds good for sins against unity. Hence the Council in a spirit of humility and prayer begs pardon of God and of our separated brethren just as we forgive those who trespass against us. The decree states that such a change of heart and holiness of life, along with public and private prayer for the unity of Christians, should be regarded as the soul of the ecumenical movement.

The Council encourages Catholics to pray among themselves for unity and on suitable occasions to join with their separated brethren in such prayers. But worship in common with them is not to be regarded as a means to be used indiscriminately for the achievement of Christian unity. Why? Because the official, formal worship of a Church normally implies commitment to the faith or creed of that specific Church. Nevertheless the decree positively encourages some worship in common with Eastern Churches because the Council recognizes the same priesthood and Eucharist in those Churches and the Catholic Church.

It is necessary for Catholics, points out the decree, to acquire an adequate understanding of the respective doctrines of our separated brethren, their spiritual and liturgical life, their history, psychology and cultural background. For this purpose meetings of both sides should be arranged for the discussion of theological problems, with each side speaking with candor and listening attentively to each other. In schools and seminaries theology and other branches of knowledge, especially history, should be taught from the ecumenical point of view.

Catholics and other Christians should cooperate in community affairs and thus manifest vividly the bond already uniting them. This is particularly necessary in regions where a social and technical evolution is taking place. Such collaboration contributes to the proper appreciation of the dignity of the human person, to the advancement of peace and the promotion of the arts and sciences in a truly Christian spirit. It should be intensified to relieve famine and natural disasters, illiteracy, poverty, lack of housing and unequal distribution of wealth.

Discussing the Churches separated from the Roman Apostolic See, the Council calls attention to the many doctrines and traditions held in common with the Churches springing from the Reformation and particularly with Anglicans. It acknowledges the special position of the Eastern Churches, many of which trace their origins to the Apostles. From the treasury of these ancient Churches the Church of the West has drawn generously for its liturgy, spiritual tradition and jurisprudence. Indeed not a few of the basic dogmas of the Christian faith concerning the Trinity and the incarnate Word were defined in ecumenical councils held in the East.

The Eastern Churches

The Eastern Christians celebrate the sacred liturgy, especially the Eucharistic mystery, source of the Church's life and pledge of future glory. Through the celebration of this mystery in each of these Churches, the Church of God is built up and grows in stature. Although separated from us, these Churches possess true sacraments, above all—by apostolic succession—the priesthood and the Eucharist, whereby they are still joined to us in closest intimacy. Hence in suitable circumstances and with the approval of Church authority, some form of worship in common is not merely possible but is encouraged.

Moreover, from the days of the early Fathers a monastic spiritual-ity flourished in the East and later flowed over into the West. Hence the Council recommends Catholics to avail themselves more fre-quently of the spiritual riches of the Eastern Fathers. It is of su-preme importance to understand, venerate, preserve and foster the rich liturgical and spiritual heritage of the Eastern Churches in order to preserve the fullness of Christian tradition and thus to bring about reconciliation between the Eastern and Western Chris-tians.

A diversity of discipline and of customs among the Eastern Churches has been sanctioned from the earliest times by synods and even by ecumenical councils. Accordingly the Council solemnly assures the Eastern Churches that, keeping in mind the necessary unity of the whole Church, they have the authority to govern them-selves according to their own disciplines. These are better suited to the character of their faithful and better adapted to foster their spiritual growth. The perfect observance of this traditional principle is a prerequisite for any restoration of unity.

East and West have used different methods and approaches in the study of revealed truth and have expressed that truth in various formulations. These are often to be considered as complementary rather than conflicting. Many of the Eastern children of the Catholic Church are preserving their heritage by living in full communion with their brethren who follow the tradition of the West. While grateful for this, the Council declares that "this entire heritage of spirituality and liturgy, of discipline and theology, in their various traditions, belongs to the full Catholic and Apostolic character of the Church" (# 17).

In view of all these facts the Council confirms what previous Councils and popes have proclaimed: in order to restore communion and unity or preserve them, one must "impose no burden beyond what is indispensable" (Acts 15:28). The Council expresses the urgent desire that every effort should be made toward the gradual realization of this unity in the various organizations and living ac-tivities of the Church, particularly by fraternal dialogue on doctrine and pastoral problems of our time.

The decree recommends that the pastors and faithful of the Cath-olic Church in the West establish close relations with those of the

East now living in their midst, so that friendly collaboration with them may increase in a spirit of love, without bickering or rivalry. If this is done wholeheartedly the Council hopes that, with the removal of the wall that has so long divided the Eastern and Western Church, "there may be but one dwelling, firmly established on the cornerstone, Christ Jesus, who will make both one" (# 18).

Dialogue with Western Churches

The Council then turns its attention to the separated Churches in the West, springing from the Reformation or later events. They have many ties with the Catholic Church as a result of the long span of earlier centuries when the Christian people had lived in ecclesiastical communion. Hence, in spite of weighty differences of a historical, sociological, psychological and cultural character, and especially in the interpretation of revealed truth, the Council suggests some considerations which can serve as a basis and encouragement for a dialogue.

(1) Many of the separated Churches acknowledge Jesus Christ as God and Lord and as the only mediator between God and man for the glory of the one God, the Father, the Son and the Holy Spirit. They look to Christ as the source and center of ecclesiastical communion. Their longing for union with Christ prompts them to seek unity and to bear witness to their faith among the nations of the world.

(2) The Gospel "is the power of God for salvation to everyone who has faith, to the Jew first and then to the Greek" (Rom. 1:16). A reverence for and love of Holy Scripture impels our separated brethren to a constant and diligent study of the sacred text. Here they contemplate the life of Christ and become familiar with His teachings and actions, particularly the mysteries of His death and resurrection.

(3) While our separated brethren affirm the divine authority of the Bible, they differ from us about the relationship of the Scriptures and the Church. Despite such divergence, the sacred Word in the dialogue is a precious instrument in the mighty hand of God for the achievement of that unity, for which the divine Redeemer prayed so earnestly on the night before He died on Calvary's Cross.

"For you were buried," says the Apostle Paul, "together with Him in baptism, and in Him also arose again through faith in the working of God who raised him from the dead" (Col. 2:12). Accordingly whenever baptism is conferred in the way Christ determined and is received with proper dispositions of soul, a person becomes truly incorporated into the crucified and glorified Christ and is reborn to a sharing in the divine life. Hence baptism is only a beginning; it is the first step toward a complete incorporation into the system of salvation as Christ willed it to be and finally toward a complete integration into Eucharistic communion.

Our separated brethren lack the fullness of union with us which flows from baptism and, we believe, have not preserved the proper reality of the Eucharistic mystery in its fullness, especially because of the absence of the sacrament of orders. Nevertheless when they commemorate the Lord's death and resurrection in the Holy Supper, they acknowledge that it signifies life in communion with Christ and await His coming in glory. Hence the doctrine about the Lord's Supper, about the other sacraments, worship and ministry in the Church should form profitable subjects of dialogue.

The Christian way of life of these brethren is nourished by faith and strengthened by the grace of baptism and the hearing of the word of God. They engage in private prayer, in meditation on the Scriptures, and they assemble in the worship of God. They manifest a lively sense of justice and a true charity toward others. Inspired by their Christian faith, they have established many organizations for the relief of spiritual and material distress, the futherance of education, the betterment of society and the promotion of peace.

While our separated brethren differ with us in some applications of the Gospel to modern society, they strive to cling to Christ's word as the source of Christian virtue and to obey the command of the Apostles: "Whatever you do in word or in work, do all in the name of the Lord Jesus, giving thanks to God the Father through him" (Col. 3:17). Hence the ecumenical dialogue could profitably start with the moral application of the Gospel.

After setting forth the conditions under which ecumenical activity may be practiced and the principles by which it is to be guided, the Council hopes that the initiative of her children joined with that of the separated brethren will advance without obstructing the ways of divine Providence and without prejudging the future inspirations of the Holy Spirit. The Council realizes that the reconciliation of all Christians in the unity of the one Church of Christ transcends human power. Accordingly it places its hopes entirely in the prayer of Christ for the Church, in the love of the Father for us, and in the power of the Holy Spirit. The decree ends by recalling the assuring words of the Apostle Paul: "And hope does not disappoint because God's love has been poured forth in our hearts through the Holy Spirit who has been given to us" (Rom. 5:5).

Church Unity Octave

During the Church Unity Octave, January 18 to 25, in 1966, the Christian world witnessed turnouts of Protestants and Catholics at prayer services for unity on an unprecedented scale. In thousands of towns and throughout cities in the U.S. such services were held in Catholic churches with the priest leading the devotions and the Protestant minister preaching the homily and in Protestant churches with the roles of priest and minister reversed. The large attendance of the laity of both Churches and the fervor with which they participated were indeed heart-warming and hopefully an augury of still greater developments.

Dialogues between theological experts and between pastors of both groups are being held with increasing frequency in all parts of the country. They begin cautiously and a bit timidly until they get to know one another and see the unmistakable evidence of sincerity and good faith. Then discussion proceeds more freely, enabling each side to learn more clearly the belief, discipline, structure and worship of the various Churches represented. Such meetings have already created a new warmth and friendship among clergymen who before scarcely had a speaking acquaintance with one another.

The importance of such friendship among the clergy and their respective flocks can hardly be overestimated, for it represents the first step in the long journey to Christian unity. Friendship brings them together in prayer, and in humble and persevering petition to God lies our best and only chance for success. Such joint prayer is especially effective, for it is in accord with the words of

Christ: "Where two or three are gathered together for my sake, there am I in the midst of them" (Mt. 18:20).

On June 18, 1965, the U.S. Bishops' Commission of Ecumenical Affairs issued a statement, *Interim Guidelines for Prayer and Communicatio in Sacris*. It contains a set of recommendations based on two decrees issued by the Second Vatican Council, namely, the *Decree on Ecumenism* and the *Decree on Eastern Catholic Churches*. Frequently in the document it is noted that local bishops have the authority to decide in regard to prayer in common with members of other communions. They interpret and apply the guidelines in particular circumstances of time and place.

The Bishops' Commission for Ecumenical Affairs was established by the American hierarchy at their annual meeting in Rome in November, 1964, to interpret and implement for this country the *Decree on Ecumenism* and to propose guidelines for ecumenical dialogue and action. It also provides a point of contact with other Christian Churches, directs the dialogue with the Eastern Orthodox and serves as a liaison agency between the U.S. bishops and the Vatican Secretariat for Promoting Christian Unity.

Cardinal Shehan of Baltimore was appointed chairman of the commission, whose work on every phase of ecumenism has been portioned out among eight subcommissions. In November, 1965, the commission was enlarged from seven to fourteen bishops, and Bishop John J. Carberry of Columbus became the new chairman. Monsignor William W. Baum is the executive director. Commission headquarters are in Washington, D.C.

Guidelines for Joint Action

Due to the initiative of this commission there have been several significant developments worth noting. In Washington, D.C., on June 22, 1965, fifteen representatives of the Protestant Episcopal Church and of the Catholic Church met to discuss matters of a pastoral nature. Among these were the difficulties arising from mixed marriages and the Catholic practice of conditionally rebaptizing baptized Episcopalians received into the Church. Catholic representatives pointed out that baptism should be conferred unconditionally unless there is doubt about the validity of a former baptism.

There was general agreement that the search for Christian unity cannot be left to theological discussions alone but will have its main basis in the mutual quest for holiness and adherence to God's will.

A second meeting on the national level took place in Baltimore on July 6 and 7, when Lutheran and Catholic representatives compared their interpretations of the Nicene Creed, which is used in the Eucharistic liturgies of both Churches. A statement issued at the conclusion of the discussions noted that full inquiry has to be made of "the nature and structure of the teaching authority of the Church" and "the role of Scripture in relation to the teaching office of the Church. . . . We together acknowledge that the problem of the development of doctrine is crucial today and is in the forefront of our common concern."

A third national conference was held in Washington, D.C., on July 27, with 10 Presbyterians and 10 Catholics participating. The Presbyterian representatives were five ministers and five lay persons, of whom three were women. Representing the Catholic Church were Bishop Ernest L. Unterkoefler, six priests, two laymen and one woman. The joint communiqué issued at the end of the meeting is worth citing because it aptly depicts the present state of the ecumenical movement and the lines of its future direction.

It read as follows: "We have met today as fellow Christians, conscious both of the unity in Christ that we enjoy by virtue of a common baptism, and of the disunity as churches to which we have all contributed and for which we ask forgiveness of God and of one another. Our consultation has included both clergy and laity of the Roman Catholic and United Presbyterian Churches, as an expression of the belief we share in common in the priesthood of all the faithful. Our purpose today has not been to arrive at premature conclusions but to clarify the direction our future meetings should take. We have discovered two clear types of concerns, one focusing on theological issues that should involve us as separated Christians, the other focusing on the common task we face together as believers bearing witness to Christ before all mankind. We are sure that these concerns must not be separated from one another."

The statement continued: "We have decided that the particular thrust of our discussion will be a joint exploration of the theme of reform and renewal as a continuing process in the life of the

Church and its people. By this we hope to highlight not only man's role but also the role of the Holy Spirit, and to search for signs of His activity within the Church, within our separate and common worship, and in a fresh encounter with what He is saying to us through the voice of the secular world. For this purpose we envision that our future association will involve doctrine, worship and social action, in an ongoing search for fidelity to the Gospel of Christ."

A fourth ecumenical dialogue was held on September 9 in Worcester, where representatives of the Standing Conference of Orthodox Bishops and a Catholic subcommittee, headed by Bishop Bernard J. Flanagan, discussed steps leading toward unity. Future meetings are being arranged by the Bishop's Commission which will bring together Catholics and representatives of a variety of other Christian Churches.

"The year 1965," said Monsignor Baum, "will go down in the history of the American Catholic Church as the year when bishops became officially involved in the great task of seeking unity. This overshadows all the high-level dialogues, joint prayer services and areas of religious cooperation that were significant steps forward in relations among Christian bodies."

Three Reasons

Monsignor Baum cites three reasons for his conclusion. First, the bishops themselves are actually engaged in the dialogue. In the past the participants were almost exclusively speculative theologians. Now, in the light of Catholic teaching concerning the episcopacy, the dialogues take on new significance and importance. Secondly, the involvement of bishops as well as theologians will result in a more "pastoral" approach that will affect dioceses, parishes and lay people.

Thirdly, the bishops' participation shows the Church's desire to deal with other Christians on an *institutional* basis, Church-to-Church. We are no longer treating others merely as sincere Christians but as members of Christian Churches. This reflects the Vatican Council's recognition of the "Churchly" nature and value of these institutions.

This does not mean any lessening of the necessity, importance and value of the dialogue on the other levels, involving pastors, religious and laity. Such "grass roots" ecumenism is essential if the dialogue on the upper level is to have wide popular support and practical significance. This is evidenced by the failure of the agreements, reached at the Council of Lyons in 1274 and at the Council of Ferrara-Florence from 1438–1443, to heal the Eastern Schism.

The reasons for the agreement had not been sufficiently explained to the Christians of the East and hence it had no popular support. If the movement for Christian unity is to succeed, it must enter into the blood stream of the masses of Christian people and become a spirit-changing catalyst on the community and parish level. With this in mind, the U.S. Bishops' Commission for Ecumenical Affairs is endeavoring to have representatives of the different levels participate in the dialogues.

The ecumenical developments on all levels in the Catholic Church in the U.S. are so striking that they have attracted the attention of the people not only of this country but also of other nations. Speaking from the pulpit of Grace Episcopal Cathedral in San Francisco in 1965, the Rev. Dr. Eugene Carson Blake pointed out that recent developments in the Catholic Church make the need for non-Catholic unity efforts "more important and more urgent."

Citing the "amazing and miraculous renewal of the Catholic Church," he declared that "no Protestant dares ignore either the reality of Catholic renewal or its bearing upon the life and direction of all Christian Churches." From a keen European observer comes similar testimony. Though the involvement of the Church in the U.S. has been relatively recent, observed Father Hans Küng, it has made such giant strides that it is already beyond the Church in Europe in several areas.

These developments show how earnestly the Catholics of this country—bishops, priests, religious and laity—have responded to the appeal of the Second Vatican Council when it said: "Today in many parts of the world, under the inspiring grace of the Holy Spirit, many efforts are being made in prayer, word and action to attain that fullness of unity which Jesus Christ desires. The sacred Council exhorts, therefore, all the Catholic faithful to recognize the signs of the times and to take an active and intelligent part in the work of ecumenism" (*Decree on Ecumenism,* #4).

X.

RELIGIOUS FREEDOM FOR ALL

OF all the decrees and declarations issued by the Second Vatican Council, the one that was received with the greatest plaudits from the whole world was undoubtedly the Declaration on Religious Freedom. In the U.S. with its hundreds of religious faiths the proclamation was welcomed with especial enthusiasm. Among not a few of our citizens there had been the feeling that the Catholic Church was keen for religious liberty in countries in which her members constituted a marked minority but far from enthusiastic for it where they were a majority, as in Spain and Italy. Hence the Council discussions on this theme were followed here with unusual interest.

The initial text of the declaration was discussed and debated at great length in numerous meetings of the Council. Cardinals Meyer, Spellman, Cushing and Ritter, the leaders of the U.S. bishops, spoke vigorously for a forthright unequivocal statement upholding the religious freedom of every man. Virtually none of the Council members was actually opposed to the principle of religious liberty; indeed some suggested that a short concise statement approving it be issued at once. Such was the suggestion of Archbishop Pietro Parente of Italy, with which Cardinal Ritter and others agreed.

Others wanted to be sure, however, that the statement make clear that this was not to be construed as an endorsement of religious indifference or of the lack of any objective basis for religious truth. Some feared that individuals might construe it as an invitation to concoct their own creeds out of their subjective fancies and to discard completely the authority of both the Church and the Bible. It soon became clear, however, that, if the pronouncement on a subject embittered by many centuries of political strife and religious controversy, were to be meaningful, it would be necessary to set forth its rational basis with much care and in considerable detail.

Accordingly the Council Fathers plunged into the debate with great vigor, with representatives of virtually all countries speaking. The chief spokesman for the declaration was Bishop Joseph De Smedt of Bruges, Belgium, who explained and defended the schema on repeated appearances before the Council. On each occasion he was warmly applauded. The American part in drafting the declaration was pre-eminently the work of Father John Courtney Murray, S.J., an international authority on Church-State relations and generally considered the declaration's chief architect.

It appeared certain that the declaration would be ratified before the close of the third session since it had already been approved by an overwhelming majority. But a few of the Council members demanded time for still more discussion, and they were upheld by Cardinal Eugene Tisserant, the Council moderator. Though an estimated thousand members, under the leadership of Cardinal Albert Meyer, hurriedly appealed to Pope Paul VI to overrule that decision, their appeal was denied. Thus the session ended on a note of disappointment, frustration and chagrin.

After further lengthy discussion at the fourth session and further revision of the text, the declaration was finally approved by a vote of 1,934 to 249 on November 19, 1965, and was subsequently promulgated by Pope Paul VI. Because of the great significance and the exceptional timeliness of this historic document we shall present not only its highlights but also all its important points.

No Espousal of Indifferentism

To preclude the misconception that the Church, in upholding the right of every person to religious freedom, was espousing religious indifferentism, the Council affirms its belief that God Himself has revealed to mankind the way in which they are to worship and serve Him and thus attain eternal life. To transmit that revelation to all men, Christ founded the Catholic and Apostolic Church when He said to the Apostles: "Go, therefore, and make disciples of all nations, baptizing them in the name of the Father and of the Son and of the Holy Spirit, teaching them to observe all things whatsoever I have commanded you; and behold, I am with you all days even to the consummation of the world" (Mt. 28:18-20). Hence all men are obliged to seek the truth, especially in what concerns God and His Church, and to embrace the truth they come to know, and to hold fast to it.

The Council expresses its belief that these obligations exert their binding force upon the human conscience; that truth cannot impose itself except by virtue of its own truth, as it enters into the mind quietly and with power. Religious freedom has to do with immunity from coercion in civil society and hence leaves untouched traditional Catholic doctrine on the moral duty of men and societies toward the true religion and toward the one Church of Christ.

After these introductory remarks, the Council asserts that every person has a right to religious freedom. This means that all men are to be immune from coercion on the part of individuals, social groups or any human power in such wise that no one is to be coerced to act contrary to his own beliefs, either privately or publicly, either alone or in association with others, within due limits.

The Basis of Religious Liberty

What is the basis of such a right? It is the dignity of the human person as this dignity is known through the revealed word of God and by reason itself. Furthermore this right is to be acknowledged in the constitutional law whereby society is governed and thus is to become a civil right. Hence the right to religious freedom has its basis not in the subjective disposition of the individual but in his very nature.

Consequently the right to this immunity continues to exist even in those who do not live up to their obligation of seeking the truth and embracing it, and the exercise of this right is not to be impeded, provided that just public order be observed. While error as such does not possess rights, the erring individual still retains the right to religious freedom because of the dignity of his human nature.

The highest norm of human life is the divine law, eternal, objective and universal, whereby God orders, directs and governs the entire universe and all the ways of the human community by a plan conceived in wisdom and love. Man has been fashioned by God to participate in this law with the consequence that, under the gentle disposition of divine Providence, he can come to perceive ever more fully the truth that is unchanging. Hence every individual has the obligation, and therefore the right, to seek the truth in religious matters so that he may with prudence form for himself right and true judgments of conscience, using all suitable means.

Through the mediation of conscience man perceives and acknowledges the imperatives of the divine law. In all his actions he is obliged to follow his conscience so that he may come to God, the end and purpose of life. Hence he is not to be coerced to act contrary to his conscience, nor is he to be prevented from following it, especially in religious matters. Why? Because the exercise of religion, of its very nature, consists primarily in the internal, voluntary and free acts whereby man sets the course of his life directly toward God. No human power may either command or forbid acts of this kind.

Man's Social Nature

Man has, however, a social nature. This requires him to give external expression to his internal acts of religion: to share with others in religious matters and to profess his religion in community. Consequently injury is done to the human person and to the very order established by God for human life, if the free exercise of religion is prohibited in society, provided just public order is observed.

Religious communities are a requirement of the social nature of man and of religion itself. Wherefore they have the right to freedom so that they may govern themselves according to their own norms, honor almighty God in public worship and their members in practicing the religious life, strengthen them by instruction and promote institutions in which they may join together to order their own lives in accordance with their religious principles.

The declaration then takes up the matter of family rights. Since the family is a society in its own original right, points out the document, it has the right freely to live its own domestic religious life under the guidance of parents. The latter have the right to determine the kind of religious education which their children are to receive.

Civil authority must, therefore, recognize the right of parents to make a genuinely free choice of schools and of other means of education; the exercise of this freedom of choice is not to be made a reason for imposing unjust burdens on parents, either directly or indirectly. Furthermore the rights of parents are violated, if their children are compelled to attend classes or instructions which are contrary to their religious beliefs, or if a single system of education, from which all religious formation is excluded, is imposed upon all.

Upon whom does the care of the right to religious freedom rest? It rests upon the whole citizenry, social groups, government, the Church and other religious communities in virtue of the duty of all and in the manner proper to each. Since the protection of the inviolable rights of man ranks among the fundamental duties of government, it is bound to safeguard the religious freedom of all its citizens in an effective manner by just laws and other appropriate means.

A Sensitive Area

The declaration then comes into the sensitive area where a particular faith is officially recognized as the state religion, as in England, Italy, Sweden and Spain. The document asserts that in such cases it is imperative that the right of all citizens and religious communities to religious freedom should be recognized and made effective in practice. Hence a wrong is done when the civil authority imposes upon its citizens, by force or fear, the profession or repudiation of any religion, or when it prohibits men from joining or leaving a religious community. It is a grievous violation of the will of God, of the sacred rights of the person and of the family of nations when force is used to repress or destroy religion, either in the whole of mankind or in a particular country or in a definite community.

Is the exercise of the right to religious freedom subject to certain regulatory norms? Yes, says the declaration. In the use of all freedoms the moral principle of personal and social responsibility is to be observed. In exercising their rights, individuals and social groups are obliged by the moral law to have respect both for the rights of others and for their own duties toward others and for the general welfare.

Moreover, society has the right to defend itself against abuses committed under the pretext of freedom of religion. Hence a proper appreciation of religious liberty should prompt men to act with greater responsibility in fulfilling their duties in community life.

Freedom Is Rooted in Divine Revelation

The Council points out that the doctrine of religious freedom has its roots in divine revelation and hence Christians should respect it conscientiously. While revelation does not affirm in explicit language the right of man to immunity from external coercion in religious matters, it discloses the dignity of man in its full dimensions and evidences the respect which Christ showed toward this freedom.

One of the major tenets of the Catholic faith is that man's response to God in faith must be free: no one therefore is to be compelled to embrace the Christian faith against his will. This doctrine is contained in holy Scripture and in the writings of the Fathers of the Church. Consequently the principle of religious liberty contributes mightily to the creation of an environment in which men can without hindrance be invited to the Christian faith, embrace it voluntarily, and profess effectively in their life.

In His earthly life Christ set us an inspiring example of respecting the conscience of men. Meek and humble of heart, Jesus won by the beauty and goodness of His life and by His miracles the free allegiance of men. Noting that cockle had been sown amid the wheat, He gave orders that both should be allowed to grow until the harvest time, which will be at the end of the world.

Disdaining the role of a political messiah ruling by force, He preferred to be known as the Son of man, who came "to serve and to give his life a ransom for the many" (Mk. 10:45). Wishing His disciples to follow His example of humility and meekness, Jesus said: "Learn from me, for I am meek and humble of heart" (Mt. 11:29). His mercy and compassion won the hearts of sinners and brought tears of repentance to their eyes. He was the true servant of God, who "does not break the bruised reed nor extinguish the smoking flax" (Mt. 12:20).

The Example of Christ

Jesus acknowledged the authority of government and its rights when He ordered tribute be rendered to Caesar, but He warned that the higher rights of God are to be kept inviolate: "Render to Caesar the things that are Caesar's and to God the things that are God's" (Mt. 22:21).

While Jesus always bore witness to the truth, He steadfastly refused to impose it by force upon the unconvinced and the unwilling. His rule is established by witnessing to the truth and by hearing the truth, and it extends its reign over the minds and hearts of men by the love whereby Christ, lifted up on the cross, draws all men to Himself.

Walking in the footsteps of the divine Master, the Apostles and disciples strove to win men to the faith not by coercion but by the inherent power of the word of God. Steadfastly they proclaimed the Gospl of our Lord, "who wills that all men should be saved and come to the acknowledgment of the truth" (1 Tim. 2:4). At the same time, however, they respected those in error, thus making it clear that "each one of us is to render to God an account of himself" (Rom. 14:12), and hence is to follow his conscience.

Fully convinced that the Gospel is indeed the power of God unto salvation for all who believe, they spoke "the word with confidence" (Acts 4:13) before the people and their rulers. Spurning all "carnal weapons" like their gentle Master, the Apostles proclaimed the word of God in the profound conviction that there is inherent in this word a mysterious divine power capable of conquering all opposition and of bringing men to faith in Christ and in His service.

Following the example of Jesus, the Apostles recognized legitimate civil authority. "For there is no power except from God," the Apostle Paul teaches, and thereafter commands: "Let everyone be subject to higher authorities . . . He who resists authority resists God's ordinance" (Rom. 13:1-5). Nevertheless they did not hesitate to speak out against governing powers which set themselves in opposition to the ordinances of God: "It is necessary to obey God rather than men" (Acts 5:29). Such is the path in which the martyrs, saints and sages of the Christian faith have walked through all ages and over all the earth.

The Church is walking in their footsteps and in those of Christ Jesus, when it proclaims the principle of religious freedom as befitting the dignity of man and as being in accord with divine revelation. This has always been an integral part of her faith even though, through the vicissitudes of human history, there were times when this principle, like the other directives of Christ, was violated. In spite of such abuses, the doctrine of the Church that no one is to be coerced into faith has always stood as firm as the Rock of Gibraltar.

To minister effectively to the hundreds of millions of her children in all the countries of the world, the Church herself must retain the freedom with which He endowed her and which He purchased with His blood. To strive to deprive her of that freedom is to flaunt the will of God. Hence the freedom of the Church is the fundamental principle underlying all her relations with governments and the whole civil and political order.

Independence Is Necessary

Such independence from the secular arm is necessary for the fulfillment of her divine mission. So too do the Christian faithful, in common with all other men, possess the civil right not to be hindered in leading their lives in accordance with their consciences. Consequently a wholesome and mutually helpful harmony exists between the liberty of the Church and the religious freedom which is to be recognized as the right of all men and communities and sanctioned by constitutional law.

The Council then turns its attention to the Church's own children. It earnestly requests them to assist their Holy Mother to fulfill the divine command to "teach all nations" and to work with all urgency "that the word of God be spread abroad and glorified" (2 Thess. 3:1). It earnestly begs of its children that, "first of all, supplications, prayers, petitions, acts of thanksgiving be made for all men . . . For this is good and agreeable in the sight of God our Saviour, who wills that all men be saved and come to the knowledge of the truth" (1 Tim. 2:1-4).

Since by the will of God, the Church is the teacher of divine truth, the Christian faithful ought carefully to attend to the sacred and certain doctrine of the Church. To her has been given the authority to teach the truth which is Christ Himself and to make clear those principles of the moral order which have their origins in human nature itself. Hence the disciple of Christ should strive ever more fully to understand the truth revealed by Him, faithfully to proclaim it and vigorously to defend it, but always by means consonant with the spirit of the Gospel.

The Council looks with joy upon the religious freedom that has already been declared a civil right in most constitutions and recognized in international documents. It looks with sorrow, however, upon the actions of a government which, while professing in its constitutions freedom of worship, deters its citizens from exercising that freedom and even seeks to eradicate religious faith from its youth.

Constitutional Guarantee of Freedom Needed

The Council pleads with all men to consider how necessary religious liberty is, especially today when nations are coming into ever closer unity and men of different religions and cultures are being brought into closer relationships. There is an increasing realization of the personal responsibility incumbent upon every man to safeguard and promote this liberty. "Consequently," says the Council, "in order that relationships of peace and harmony be established within the whole of mankind, it is necessary that freedom be everywhere provided with an effective constitutional guarantee and that respect be shown for the high duty and right of man freely to lead his religious life in society."

The declaration then closes with the following brief but moving prayer: "May the God and Father of all grant that the human family, through careful observance of the principle of religious freedom in society, may be brought by the grace of Christ and the power of the Holy Spirit to the sublime and unending and glorious 'freedom of the sons of God' (Rom. 8:21)."

Never before in all history have the grounds for religious freedom in both reason and divine revelation been worked out with such penetration, care and thoroughness. The declaration will stand as an impregnable bastion of religious liberty and the rights of conscience against all assaults as long as the human race survives upon this planet.

XI.

THE CHURCH: PEOPLE OF GOD

THE *Constitution on the Church* has been been widely acclaimed as the chief accomplishment of the Second Vatican Council. It carried to completion the work of the First Vatican Council by setting forth in detail the role of bishops and the relationships between them and the pope in the hierarchical structure of the Church. Adopted before most of the other enactments of the Council, the constitution served as the basic document with which all other decrees and actions of the synod were harmonized.

True to the pastoral and ecumenical spirit of the Council, the constitution contains no new definitions of faith or fresh anathemas. Although it reflects the Church's highest teaching authority, it does not say the last word on any of the doctrines discussed because the Council did not wish to close the door to future developments and new charismatic insights into God's Word.

While the definition of a doctrine is sometimes necessary, every new definition sets up an additional roadblock on the boulder-strewn path of those approaching the Church from outside. Christians are now not only more painfully conscious of the need for unity but are also striving for it on a worldwide scale never equalled before. Mindful that the post-Tridentine definitions of papal infallibility, the immaculate conception and the assumption of the Blessed Virgin have increased the difficulty of Catholic ecumenism, the Council Fathers evidently did not wish at this critical juncture to set up additional obstacles.

The constitution depicts the Church in her earthly pilgrimage as primarily the spiritual fellowship of her baptized members, the People of God, and only secondarily as a juridical hierachical institution. The role of the pope, the other bishops, priests and religious is portrayed as essentially one of humble, devoted and self-effacing service for God's people.

The charismatic gifts, which have constituted the dynamic cata-lystic element in the Church's life, are bestowed, points out the Council, on clergy and laity alike. The note of triumphalism, which has so often been overemphasized to the detriment of the Church's public image, is seldom heard in this document. The discussion of problems raised by the existence of Christians not in communion with the See of Rome is uniformly respectful and friendly, and thus sets the tone for the *Decree on Ecumenism.*

History of the Constitution

A schema on the Church, drafted before the Council opened, was severely criticized during the first session as the superficial, trite and slavish echoing of mere seminary manuals. These had their roots back in the Counter-Reformation and in the medieval struggles be-tween Church and empire. Barren of fresh insights and of an awareness of the radically changed world in which we are living, the schema was rejected.

A new draft was submitted at the second session and was dis-cussed at great length. With the presence of representatives of the Church in the Afro-Asian countries and of the oriental Catholicism of the United Church, the Council became increasingly mindful as Abbot Basil C. Butler, O.S.B., points out, that the Church is some-thing far greater than the Western Patriarchate. This awareness was further heightened by the spokesmen of a great theological and Biblical renaissance that goes back to the pre-war years but which has increased mightily in scope and depth in the countries of North-ern Europe.

Determined to meet the demands of an age without precedent in human history, the Council Fathers realized the necessity of en-gaging in basic theological thinking and reflecting upon the nature of the Church, her functions and her mission. The constitution re-flects the results of the Council's profound and sustained thought on these fundamental topics. After prolonged debate the Fathers decided that the subject of Our Lady should be treated in a chapter of the constitution rather than in a separate document, as had originally been intended.

There is no doubt that devotion to the Blessed Virgin will gain in quality from the wise decision to keep this doctrine within the framework of the theology of her divine Son and of the Church. This would seem to be further confirmed by the new title, Mother of the Church, bestowed upon her.

Within the theological framework of the Church, of which she is both type and preeminent member, Marian devotion can be best protected from the extravagant and unseemly exhibitions, to which it is at times exposed by well meaning but improperly educated people. Cells which grow wildly and without restraint become cancerous; so too do devotions which fail to follow the guidelines provided by the Church. It is no secret that this was a matter of much concern both to the Council and to non-Catholic Christians.

Mary's Place Is Clear

Commenting on the decision to keep Marian doctrine within the constitution, Archbishop Paul J. Hallinan of Atlanta thus admirably expressed the mind of the Council: "If our Lord Jesus Christ is kept in the center of the Christian's life of prayer and worship, all other elements appear in their proper place. Surely the place of His Mother Mary was made clear by Christ Himself at the wedding feast of Cana and at Calvary, by Mary herself, and should be clear to all of us. Because she is the Mother of Christ, she has a claim upon our filial love and our proper veneration. But to attempt to center our religion in Mary, to exaggerate her cult, to multiply her devotions in such a way that Christ is obscured or forgotten would be a blasphemy to the Son, an embarrassment to the memory of the Mother and a pathetic deviation on the part of those baptized in Christ."

Like the *Constitution on the Sacred Liturgy,* this one is also profoundly Biblical in inspiration. It will be read with pleasure and profit by our separated brethren as well as by Catholics, thus facilitating the growing dialogue between both groups. The whole document stands as a monument to the revival of Biblical scholarship and theology in the Church. A comparsion of the first draft with the completely rewritten and revised one reveals the giant strides in theological *aggiornamento* taken by the Council from the time it convened on October 12, 1962, to the time of its adoption by a vote of 2,151 to 5 on November 21, 1964.

The constitution is not immediately directed to practical changes. Hence its value for the Church and the future of Christianity will hinge largely on our willingness to grasp and spread its message, and to give practical expression to its implications. Its key doctrines are: the common priesthood of all the faithful, resulting from their baptism; the intrinsic life of the local Church, centered in the Eucharist; the ministerial priesthood and episcopate; and the collegial authority and responsibilities of the bishops within the hierarchical communion of the Church.

We shall present the highlights of this document as simply and briefly as possible along with some observations on it. In doing this we shall draw often upon the excellent *Commentary on the Constitution on the Church* by Father Gregory Baum, a theological expert at the Council and a member of the Secretariat for Promoting Christian Unity.

The Mystery of the Church

While the Church is a community of men with structure and laws, it is primarily the presence of God's merciful action among men. This is what the Council means by mystery. In the visible community we encounter the God of salvation, who diffuses His mercy, forgiveness and vivifying grace among us. The constitution outlines the action of the Father, Son and Spirit throughout history and their triune action in our day in sanctifying and saving a chosen People.

What happened to the millions of people who lived before the time of Christ and were outside the People of Israel? While the details of God's plan for such people have not been revealed to us, the Scriptures depict God as a God of love, who wills that all men should find life in Him. "God the Father," says the constitution, "did not leave to themselves the men fallen in Adam, but ceaselessly offered helps to salvation for the sake of Christ the Redeemer.

. . . At all times and in every nation God has given welcome to whomever fears him and does what is right." Hence we may hold that the compassion and love of God, manifest in the Church, are also active among those who have never heard of Christ or have misunderstood and therefore rejected His teachings.

The Church brings to us the mediation of Christ and the gifts of the Holy Spirit enabling us to grow in holiness and to live as children of the Father in the family of God. As often as the Eucharistic sacrifice is offered at the altar, the work of redemption is carried on. In the partaking of the Eucharistic bread the unity of all believers who constitute one body in Christ is both symbolized and effected.

The mystery of the Church was evidenced in its very foundation, when the Lord Jesus directed it to proclaim the glad tidings of salvation to all men and promised to be with it all days. After His resurrection He poured out on His disciples the Spirit promised by the Father. The Spirit will recall to the Church all things revealed to it by its Founder.

The inner nature of the Church is disclosed to us in different images. The Church is a *sheepfold* whose one and indispensable door is Christ. It is a *flock* watched over by Christ, the Good Shepherd and the Prince of Shepherds, who gave His life for His sheep. The Church is a parcel of land to be cultivated, the *tillage* of God. The Church is the *building* of God, of which Christ is the stone rejected by the builders but which has become the cornerstone.

The Church is "that Jerusalem which is above." It is also called "our mother." It is described as the spotless *spouse* of the spotless Lamb, whom Jesus "loved and for whom He delivered Himself up that He might sanctify her." The Church is the "body of Christ." We are the members of that body and Christ is the Head.

A Shift of Emphasis

Here we note, as Father Baum points out, a shift of emphasis that has occurred since *Mystici Corporis* of Pius XII, who identified, without any qualifications, the Mystical Body with the Catholic Church. Instead of doing this, the constitution declares more carefully that the Church of Christ "subsists in" the Catholic Church. While the Mystical Body and the Catholic Church are not two distinct realities, they are two distinct aspects of one and the same complex reality. In other words, the body of our Lord is in the Catholic Church but, without losing its historical and incarnate character, transcends it.

"This is important in understanding the relation of other Christians and other Christian Churches to this Church of Christ," Father Baum observes. "The transcendence of Christ's mystical body beyond the historical limits of the Catholic Church permits chapter II to say that other Christians are incorporated into the Church of Christ and offers theological justification for regarding other Christian Churches as realizations, albeit institutionally defective, of the Church of Christ." The Catholic faith teaches that the Catholic Church is the only perfect embodiment of the Church on earth but, because of the transcendence of Christ's Church, this does not preclude the possibility of partial realizations of this Church among men.

A similar distinction should be made between the Catholic Church and the Kingdom of God on earth. The latter is the dominion of almighty God and the execution of His salvific will, which is made visible especially in the person of Jesus Christ Himself who came "to serve and to give His life as a ransom for many." Like its Founder, the Church proclaims and serves this Kingdom and strives to spread it among all peoples. Because of Christ's presence in the Church, it may be regarded as the seed and the initial budding forth of this Kingdom on earth.

The People of God

The Constitution points out that God does not sanctify and save men merely as individuals, with no bond between them, but brings them together as one people who acknowledge and serve Him in holiness. God chose Israel as a people, with whom He formed a covenant, and made Himself and His decree known to them through the centuries of their history. This was done by way of preparation and as a figure of that new and perfect covenant, which was to be ratified in Christ, and of that fuller revelation which was to be given through the incarnate Son of God.

Jesus, the universal Redeemer, fulfilled the promises made to Israel, and established a new covenant, calling together both Jews and Gentiles, and making them one not according to the flesh but in the Spirit. This was the People of God, whom Christ established as "a chosen race, a royal priesthood, a holy nation, a purchased people . . . who in times past were not a people, but are now the people of God" (1 Pet. 2:9–10).

The new Israel is called the Church of Christ because He purchased it with His blood, filled it with His Spirit and provided it with the means which befit it as a visible and social union. All its members accept Jesus as the author of salvation and the source of unity and peace. Thus the Church is the visible sacrament of this saving unity. Transcending all limits of time and race, the Church extends to all regions of the earth and thus enters into the history of mankind.

Despite Christ's presence among His people, the Church remains a pilgrim community, subject to trial, tribulation and weakness of the flesh. Unlike previous ecclesiastical documents, the constitution does not hesitate to acknowledge that we, personally and corporately, fail at times to live up to our calling. The Church is holy because God is faithful to His promises, not because men are steadfast. Consequently the Church "holy and always in need of being purified, continually follows the way of penance and renewal." In short, the human element, which always looms up so prominently in the Church, is always subject to renewal and reform.

Through regeneration and the anointing of the Holy Spirit the baptized share in the priesthood of Christ. This means that all Christians have access to the Father in Christ and are able to participate in the entire liturgical life of the Church. Founded on the sacrament of orders, the liturgy exists as a ministry for the baptized, rendering more effective and Christ-centered the exercise of their common priesthood.

"Therefore," says the constitution, "all the disciples of Christ, persevering in prayer and praising God, should present themselves as a living sacrifice, holy and pleasing to God. Everywhere on earth they must bear witness to Christ and give an answer to those who seek an account of that hope of eternal life which is in them."

Who Belongs to the Church?

Who belongs to God's people? Who is incorporated into this Church? The simple answer proposed by Pius XII in *Mystici Corporis* that members of Christ's Church are really only Roman Catholics no longer holds. The constitution on the Church declares that the Catholic faithful who possess the Holy Spirit are "fully" incorporated in the Church. The change from "really" to "fully" is of profound significance. Repeatedly the constitution acknowledges that baptism incorporates men into the Church thus indicating that there are different degrees and ways of belonging to it.

Since Catholics have available to them the effective means in the form of doctrines, sacraments and hierarchical gifts for such incorporation, they may be said to be "fully" incorporated into the People of God. As Father Baum says, "This leaves room for less perfect incorporation in the Church, less perfect because the gifts available are not complete (this applies to non-Catholic Christians) or, more gravely because of the absence of the Holy Spirit and an unconverted heart (this may apply to all Christians)."

It is worth noting that the term "member" or "membership" in the Church is not used in Chapter II. The Council deemed the notion of member, analogically derived from the human body, was not adequate or useful in describing the complex relationship here involved. In the previous chapter the constitution declared that the Church of Christ transcends the Catholic Church, though forming one complex reality with, and embracing in various ways, persons baptized in other Churches. On this carefully laid groundwork Chapter II is in a position to make strong statements on non-Catholic Christians, the like of which have never appeared in any previous ecclesiastical documents.

Joined as Brothers

It declares that separated Christians are joined to us as brothers, that we share with them the gift of the Spirit. Furthermore, we share with them some or many of the elements which together build up the Church of Christ. While we believe that their Churches do not have the structure that Christ willed the Church to have, we gladly acknowledge that, despite our separation, we do have real, though limited, communion with them in the Holy Spirit.

Moreover, the Council frankly avows the operation of the Holy Spirit even beyond the Christian family created through faith and baptism. The grace of God touches the hearts of people who do know the good tidings of Christ and, if under the influence of grace, they endeavor to be faithful to the truth as they see it and live according to their conscience, they are on the way to life eternal. Whatever is good or true in other religions is traceable not simply to human efforts, but to God who enlightens all men that they may have life everlasting.

Upon every disciple of Christ, according to his state, there is imposed the obligation of spreading the faith. Echoing perennially in the Church's memory are the words of Christ: "Go, therefore, and make disciples of all nations . . ." Accordingly the Church never ceases to labor and pray that the whole human race may become the People of God, the body of the Lord and the temple of the Holy Spirit, and that in Christ, the Head of all, all honor, homage, praise and glory may be rendered to the Creator of the universe and the Father of all mankind.

The Episcopate

Treating of the hierarchical structure of the Church and particularly of the episcopate, the constitution develops the doctrine of episcopal collegiality which is the central thesis in the constitution and the peak achievement of the whole Vatican Council II. This doctrine means that the bishops of the Catholic Church in union with the supreme pontiff, the bishop of Rome, constitute a unified college or body, which is the continuation of the body of the Twelve, the Apostles with Peter as their head, which Christ made the foundation and pillars of the Church. Hence, with and under the leadership of the pope, the successor of St. Peter, the bishops collectively as successors to the Apostles, share the pastoral care and responsibility for the whole Church.

After lengthy discussion and debate, in which bishops from all the countries of the world participated, the Council finally agreed upon the following meticulously worded statement of this key doctrine: "Just as in the Gospel, the Lord so disposing, St. Peter and the other Apostles constitute one apostolic college, so in a similar way the Roman pontiff, the successor of St. Peter, and the bishops, the successors of the Apostles, are joined together. . . .

"The individual bishops, who are placed in charge of particular churches, exercise their pastoral government over the portion of the People of God committed to their care, and not over other churches nor over the universal Church. But each of them, as a member of the episcopal college and legitimate successor of the Apostles, is obliged by Christ's instiution and command to be solicitous for the whole Church, and this solicitude, though it is not exercised as an act of jurisdiction, contributes to the advantage of the universal Church."

The practical implications of this doctrine are of enormous importance. In the modern era the highly centralized governmental structure of the Church, with the Roman Curia as its chief administrative arm, has not enabled bishops to exercise the co-responsibility which is theirs by sacramental and divine right. Hence there is an urgent and crying need for a reform of the governmental structure, that will establish organs through which bishops will confer among themselves and with the pope regarding teaching and all important legislation for the universal Church.

That the cardinals and bishops of the Curia will no longer be the sole counsellors of the pope, nor have the sole responsibility for communicating the Church's policy to the Catholic people, is evident from Pope Paul VI's announcement of his intention to establish a senate or synod whose members will be chosen form the episcopacy of many lands. This will help to restore the mark of Catholicity, which has been so badly obscured by the dominance of a single national group in the Curia, in the college of cardinals and in the diplomatic corps. Only when the Church in all countries is represented in those three bodies in some reasonable proportion to the number of its participating members, will its true international character become manifest to all the world.

How is the episcopacy created in the Church? It is, the constitution declares, through sacramental consecration that a man receives the episcopate, which is the fullness of the ministerial priesthood given by Christ to the Church. Hence the episcopal ministry is not created by a juridical or legislative act but stems from the sacramental gift of orders.

As there is no episcopal college without the pope, Father Baum points out, so there is no pope without the episcopal college, for they are sacramentally inseparable. Because of his primacy the pope remains *canonically* or *juridically* independent of the episcopal college and may act at all times freely for the welfare of the universal Church. But even in so doing he is bound to the Church's episcopal structure and remains morally dependent upon it. Hence it is confidently expected that collegiality in teaching will initiate a significant and far-reaching change in the Church's practice over the last hundred years.

The chapter ends with a few paragraphs on the priesthood and diaconate. The diaconate is re-established in the Church as a permanent form of ministry, at least in the countries where the episcopate desires it and seeks the pope's approval for it. This includes the possibility of conferring the sacramental diaconate upon married men—a custom which obtained during the first thousand years of the Church's history.

The Laity

The Council next turns its attention upon the laity and points out that everything that has been previously stated in the constitution about the People of God is intended for the laity, religious and clergy alike. The term "laity" is used here to mean all the faithful except the clergy and ministers of religious orders. Through baptism the faithful are made one body with Christ and are constituted among the People of God, made sharers in the priestly, prophetic and kingly functions of Christ, and exercise this mission both in the Church and in the world.

Living in the world as they do, the laity have as their specific vocation the sanctification of the world, working in it as a leaven. In this way they can make Christ known to others, especially by the example of an upright and holy life. Christ ordered and governed His Church with a wonderful diversity, well described by St. Paul: "For just as in one body we have many members, yet all the members have not the same function, so we, the many, are one body in Christ but severally one of another" (Rom. 12:4-5).

The Chosen People of God is one: "one Lord, one faith, one baptism" (Eph. 4:5). They share a common dignity by virtue of their regeneration in Christ; they have the same filial grace and the same vocation to perfection. They possess in common one salvation, one hope and one undivided charity. Consequently there is in the Church no inequality on the basis of race, nationality, social condition or sex because "there is neither Jew nor Greek: there is neither bond nor free: there is neither male or female. For you are all one in Christ Jesus" (Gal. 3:28).

The laity, the Council says, have Christ as their brother, who came not to be served but to serve. They also have as their brothers those in the sacred ministry who by teaching, sanctifying and ruling with the authority of Christ feed the family of God so that the new commandment of love may be fulfilled by all.

The Laity Participates in Christ's Mission

The lay apostolate is a participation in the salvific mission of Christ. By virtue of their baptism and confirmation all are called to that apostolate by Christ Himself. By the sacraments, particularly the holy Eucharist, the love of God and neighbor, which is the soul of the apostolate, is communicated and nourished. The laity are summoned in a special manner to make the Church present and operative in those places and circumstances where only through them can it become the salt of the earth. Hence every layman, in virtue of the very gifts bestowed upon him, is both a witness and a living instrument of the mission of the Church itself.

In addition to this apostolate which certainly pertains to all Christians, the laity can also be called in various ways to a more direct form of cooperation in the apostolate of the hierarchy. They may have a definite role to play in the life of the Church, in liturgy and in missionary movements. Under certain circumstances they may exercise some functions that properly belong to priests and deacons such as distributing Holy Communion in crowded churches or in missions where no priest is available.

The constitution counsels bishops to listen to the laity and to use their services, especially in areas of their professional competence. While the laity should gladly obey ecclesiastical authority and help it in its mission of evangelization and sanctification, bishops should respect the freedom of the laity and allow them sufficient leeway to exercise their Christian initiative and even encourage them to find new ways in which to extend God's kingdom. Pastors should develop in their people a sense of responsibility, dedication and initiative and then inspire them to live up to their vocation as the disciples of Christ in a world desperately in need of their sanctifying ministry. In short, Christians must be to the world what the soul is to the body.

The Universal Call to Holiness

Chapter V of the constitution treats of the universal vocation to holiness in the Church. It declares that all the People of God, of whatever rank or status, are called to the fullness of the Christian life and to the perfection of charity. The Council wanted Christians to realize that sanctity must be the goal not only of the religious but also of the laymen.

To all men then living and to those still in the womb of time the Lord Jesus addressed the command: "Be you therefore perfect, even as your heavenly Father is perfect" (Mt. 5:48). Echoing the injunction of the divine Master, the Apostle Paul says: "This is the will of God, your sanctification" (1 Thess. 4:3). The perfection of which the constitution is here speaking is, in harmony with New Testament teaching, that of loving God with one's whole heart, soul and mind and in loving one's neighbor as one's self.

The constitution stresses the fact that holiness is the work of God and the fruit of the Holy Spirit in the lives of Christians. Though human cooperation is necessary at all stages in the growth in holiness, the People of God must be ever mindful that it is always God's action that renders a People pleasing unto Him. We are justified and rendered holy through faith in Jesus Christ who died on Calvary and rose from the tomb for our redemption and sanctification. We must always remember that we are sinners in need of repentance and of the merciful forgiveness gratuitously offered to those who believe.

Thus the Council declares: "The followers of Christ are called by God, not because of their works, but according to His own purpose and grace. They are justified in the Lord Jesus, because in the baptism of faith they truly become sons of God and sharers in the divine nature. In this way they are really made holy. Then too, by God's gift, they must hold on to and complete in their lives this holiness they have received . . . Since truly we all offend in many things, we all need God's mercies continually and we all must daily pray: 'Forgive us our debts.' "

The constitution is careful, Father Baum observes, to avoid the impression that holiness consists in a mechanical observance of a set of laws or a list of do's and don'ts. In the New Testament holiness is rather the conformity to the new life conferred on us in faith and baptism and nourished through the Eucharistic celebration in the community. Obedience to the Father is not a mere outward compliance with laws and regulations but is essentially an inner conversion and conformity to our divine model, the incarnate Son of God. Only when we walk in His footsteps and unite ourselves, heart, mind and soul, to Him, do we have the light of life shining within us.

The constitution makes it clear that the following of Christ does not lead one to a withdrawal from society and the world in which we live. On the contrary, holiness requires an involvement in society, prompting the Christian to struggle valiantly like a true soldier of Christ to see that the will of Christ is fulfilled in the world into which the Church has been sent. This has at times led to martyrdom which is the supreme expression of one's love.

The chapter ends by saying: "Therefore all the faithful of Christ are invited to strive for the holiness and perfection of their own proper state. Indeed they have an obligation to so strive. Let all then have care that they guide aright their own deepest sentiments of soul. Let neither the use of the things of this world nor attachment to riches, which is against the spirit of evangelical poverty, hinder them in their quest for perfect love."

Religious

The Council sets forth the principles regarding the state of life of those who profess the evangelical counsels of poverty, chastity and obedience, and dedicate themselves to the service of God, the Church, and their fellow men in religious orders or societies. While all Christians are called to follow the Lord Jesus, religious undertake to do this by definite vows or commitments not ordinarily assumed by others. These provide the religious with a firm stability in their way of life, in which they have the support of fraternal association and the counsel of superiors. The term "religious" is used here to include those drawn from the clergy and from the laity.

Among spiritual writers in the past there was a tendency, as Father Baum points out, to laud the religious life so highly that other Christians almost appeared as if they were people of lesser faith who had stopped midway on the path of perfect obedience to God. Today, when there is a better understanding and a deeper appreciation of the role of the laity, theologians discuss the special vocation to the religious life in such a way as not to belittle or disparage those who follow their baptismal vocation in the world. It is in this spirit that the Council treats this subject.

Religious life in the Church stems ultimately from Christ who by word and example gave various counsels to His people. Among these counsels tradition has singled out especially chastity dedicated to God, poverty and obedience. Over the years the Church utilized vocations to such counsels to meet the needs of Christian society and provided those thus called with various stable forms and rules for the religious life.

In explaining the origin of religious life in this manner, we assert that the inspiration for the religious life was Christ, His example and His words, while at the same time we acknowledge that the institution of religious life in the strict sense is a creation of the Church under the guidance of the Holy Spirit. Moreover it is to be noted that by attributing the so-called evangelical counsels to the "word and example" of the Lord Jesus, the Council is careful not to exclude the opinion common among contemporary theologians and Biblical scholars that the counsel of obedience is not found in the words of Scripture but is rather a form of imitating the self-effacement of the divine Redeemer who came to give His life for men.

Avoids Old Terms

It is worth noting also that the Council studiously refrains from using such traditional terms as "state of perfection" and "state of acquiring perfection." While often used in the past, these terms are theologically incorrect. Why? Because baptism itself constitutes a state of perfection—a state in which we are to live as perfect sons of God. What distinguishes the religious life from the following of the evangelical counsels in the world by the ordinary baptized Christian is its stable form of community life, approved by ecclesiastical authority and designed to intensify the imitation of Christ.

"The importance of the profession of the evaneglical counsels," says the Council, "is seen in the fact that it fosters the perfection of love of God and love of neighbor in an outstanding manner and that this profession is strengthened by vows." The Church elevates the religious profession to the dignity of a canonical state and makes clear that it is a state consecrated to God by appropriate liturgical rites. While the practice of the evangelical counsels entails the renunciation of certain values which are worthy of esteem, it does not detract from the development of the human personality but rather contributes thereto.

Religious should be devoted to the welfare of the whole Church. Hence they have the duty of working to implant and strengthen the Kingdom of Christ in souls and to extend that Kingdom in every land. Such missionary work is to be undertaken to the extent of their ability and in keeping with the proper type of their own vocation. This can be realized through prayer or the active work of the apostolate. The chapter ends by exhorting every religious to persevere in his vocation and to work and pray for the increased holiness of the Church and for the greater glory of the one and un-

divided Trinity, which in and through Christ is the fount and the
source of all holiness.

The Eschatological Nature of the Pilgrim Church

Eschatology is a branch or section of theology which deals with
the ultimate destiny or purpose of mankind and the world. Here
the constitution deals with the relations between the members of
the Church on earth, in heaven, and in the state of purification—
topics involving chiefly eschatology and the communion of saints
and our veneration of them.

It begins by telling us that the pilgrim Church on earth, of which
we are members and in which we acquire sanctity through God's
grace, will attain its full perfection only in the glory of heaven,
when there will come the time of the restoration of all things. Then
the human race and the whole world, which is closely related to
man and attains its end through him, will be perfectly re-established
in Christ.

Having been lifted up from the earth, Christ has drawn all to
Himself. After His glorious resurrection from the dead, Jesus sent
the life-giving Paraclete upon His disciples and through the Holy
Spirit established His Body, which is the Church, as the universal
sacrament of salvation. Our Lord is continually active in the world,
seeking to lead men into the Church and thereby join them to
Himself, and make them partakers of His divine life by nourishing
them with His own body and blood.

Hence the promised restoration has already begun in Christ, is
carried forward in the mission of the Holy Spirit and through Him
continues in the Church. In it we learn the meaning and purpose
of our earthly life through faith. At the same time we discharge
with hope the earthly tasks committed to us, and thus work out
our salvation. Thus Christ's purpose in announcing the future age
was not to draw the minds of men away from their present tasks
but to reveal the true meaning of our present life.

The Council reaffirms the message of the Gospel that the salvation wrought by Christ affects the destiny of a whole People,
in fact, of all mankind. With Christ's victory over sin and death,
an irreversible event has taken place in human history. That tri-

umph has ushered in a new era. Present in the risen body of the glorified Christ and at work in our lives is a new creation.

In the Church the present and the future converge. Through faith we are already hidden with Christ in God and we exult in the decisive, eschatological and irreversible triumph of the risen Redeemer. But that glorious future touches the present, for the Church in pilgrimage belongs to our day and has the appearance of this world which is passing. It is in solidarity with all men, groaning and in travail in expectation of future glory.

No Right to Isolate

It is within the context of the destiny of the whole Church and of all creation that this chapter discusses the fate of the individual. Through baptism and faith we have become the children of God and the heirs of heaven. We strive to please God and we put on His armor that we may be able to stand against the wiles of the devil and to resist in the evil day. We must follow our Lord's counsel to watch and pray lest we fall into temptation and be cast into exterior darkness where "there will be the weeping and the gnashing of teeth."

Before we reign with Christ in glory, we must stand "before the tribunal of Christ, so that each may receive what he has won through the body, according to his works, whether good or evil" (2 Cor. 5:10). At the end of the world, Jesus tells us, "they who have done good shall come forth unto resurrection of life; but those who have done evil unto resurrection of judgment" (Jn. 5:29). To help us to understand the serious consequences for weal or for woe, of the decisions we pilgrims make, our Lord announced universal redemption in terms of heaven and hell. The Church follows Christ's example and does the same.

But as Father Baum points out, preachers "have no right to isolate the mystery of heaven and hell from the total order of God's plan and present the possibility of hell as if the Gospel were a new law testing our strength and condemning us even if we believe in forgiveness. If we have the faith that God has decided to save us in Christ, then we may be sure that the God 'whose gifts and vocation are without repentance' (Rom. 11:59) will, stirring us deeply, enable us to cooperate in His work of salvation."

In terms taken from the Scriptures, the constitution describes how the members of the Church on earth are united with their brethren who have gone to rest with their Redeemer, enjoying the peace of the Father or still passing through a process of purification. They pray for us in need of succor in our pilgrimage and we pray for those who are still on the way to peace. We also pray to the members of the Church triumphant to ask for their fraternal intercession in the chorus of the entire Church.

Thus do we pilgrims look forward with faith and hope to the day when the whole Church of the saints in the supreme happiness of the beatific vision will adore God and proclaim with one voice: "To him who sits upon the throne, and to the Lamb, blessing and honor and glory and dominion forever and ever" (Apoc. 5:13).

The Blessed Virgin Mary

The constitution does not undertake to present a complete doctrine of Mary, nor does it decide matters not yet clarified. It simply sketches the role of Mary in the mystery of the incarnate Word and the Mystical Body, and the duties of redeemed mankind toward the Mother of Jesus and the Mother of men. The first section presents the role of our Lady in the economy of salvation by following the story of the Old and New Testaments so as to preclude any discrepancy between the Mother of Jesus in the Gospel, the Virgin Mary of theological manuals and the Madonna of popular devotion.

The greatest dignity bestowed on Mary is the motherhood of our Lord, which is the basis for everything said about her in the Scriptures as well as for every honor given to her in the Church. Mary's free consent at the annunciation to the birth of Jesus is the momentous event which makes her the Mother of the Son of God and justifies the praise of her as expressed in such titles as the Mother of Salvation, Mother of Life and Mother of Grace. To prepare her for this role God lavished special graces and blessings upon her, especially her immaculate conception, thus exempting her from the stain of original sin.

This section epitomizes the Gospel accounts of the birth of Jesus, the presentation in the temple, the finding of Jesus as a young boy there, the trials and consolations of Mary during the public ministry of her Son and her presence at the foot of the Cross when most of the Apostles had fled. The motherhood of Jesus is the key that explains her role in these events: it also establishes a unity between the Mother of Jesus of the Gospel, the Blessed Virgin of the theological treatises and the Madonna of popular devotion.

The second section sketches the role of the Blessed Virgin in the economy of salvation. She is proposed as "type and image" of the entire Church, as she was so closely associated with Jesus in the divine plan of salvation. All these associations must be understood, however, in the light of the basic fact that Jesus Christ is the one mediator between God and men. Hence any aid, mediation or association in spreading the work of salvation flows from, and is dependent upon, the all-sufficient and superabundant redemptive work of the divine Savior Himself.

St. Paul Speaks

It is in this sense that any use of the title "Mediatrix" applied to Mary must be understood. Indeed several cardinals and bishops had requested that such a title, which is so easily misunderstood, should not be used in regard to the Blessed Virgin. While retaining it, the Council took special pains to indicate its restricted meaning so that it does not impair or conflict in the slightest with St. Paul's oft-quoted statement: "There is one God, and one Mediator between God and men, himself man, Christ Jesus, who gave himself a ransom for all" (1 Tim. 2:5).

The Apostle's statement is so clear, unequivocal and emphatic that Jesus is the one sole Mediator between God and all mankind that no ecclesiastical authority could seriously think of minimizing and—much less—of contradicting it. Thus after quoting St. Paul's statement, the constitution declares: "The maternal duty of Mary toward men in no wise obscures or diminishes this unique mediation of Christ, but rather shows His power. For all the salvific influence of the Blessed Virgin on men originates, not from some inner necessity, but from the divine pleasure . . . In no way does it impede, but rather does it foster the immediate union of the faithful with Christ."

Among all the servants of our Savior, Mary was most intimately associated with Him through unfaltering faith, unswerving hope and fervent love. More even than the Apostles, she was faithful to her Son in fulfilling the will of the Father. Hearing the word of God and acting upon it, our Lord tells us (Lk. 8:21), is to exercise a maternal role in the Kingdom. In this sense our Lady is our Mother in the order of grace. That maternity started with the consent she gave at the annunciation, was strikingly manifest when she stood at the foot of Calvary's Cross, and it will continue until the eternal fulfillment of all the elect.

The Meaning of Mary's Titles

When she was assumed into heaven, Mary did not lay aside this salvific duty, but by her unceasing intercession continued to secure for us the gifts of eternal salvation. By her motherly love she ministers to the brethren of her Son, who still struggle amidst the dangers and temptations of this earthly life until they reach the harbor of eternal happiness. Consequently she is invoked by the Church under the titles of Advocate, Auxiliatrix, Adjutrix and Mediatrix. All these titles are to be understood, however, in such a way that they neither take away from, nor add anything to, the dignity and efficaciousness of Christ, the one Mediator.

No creature, the constitution points out, can ever be regarded as the equal of the incarnate Son of God. The priesthood of Christ is shared in various ways by the faithful and the clergy and the one goodness of God is communicated in various ways to His creatures. But this unique mediation of the divine Redeemer does not exclude but rather gives rise to a manifold cooperation which is but a sharing in this one source. Thus, by their intercession the saints and Mary, the Queen of Saints, foster a more intimate union of the faithful with our divine Lord, the one Mediator between God and man. The Lord Jesus Himself is forever responsive directly and immediately to the cry of even the least of His children.

The faithful turn their eyes to the Blessed Virgin who shines forth to the community of the elect as the Model of virtues. Devoutly meditating upon her in the light of the Word incarnate, the People of God enter more intimately into the great mystery of the Incarnation and become more and more like their Spouse.

Since her entry into salvation history the Mother of Jesus unites in herself and re-echoes the great truths of the Christian faith as she is venerated, and she brings the faithful to her Son and His sacrifice and to the love of the eternal Father.

Because of her divine maternity Mary is exalted above all the other saints of God. Though this veneration differs essentially from the worship of triune God, whom alone we adore, it will lead us, if exercised in accordance with the teachings of the Church, to greater love and adoration of God, Creator, Redeemer and Comforter of mankind. The constitution ends with the prayer that the Mother of God and the Mother of men will intercede with her divine Son that all men may be happily gathered together in peace and harmony into one People of God for the glory of the Most High and Undivided Trinity.

XII.

THE RELATION OF THE CHURCH
TO NON-CHRISTIAN RELIGIONS

ONE of the subjects discussed at great length by the Second Vatican Council, which stirred worldwide interest, was the relation of the Church to non-Christian religions. The text of the declaration, as finally adopted by the Council, was proclaimed by Pope Paul VI on October 28, 1965. We shall present all its important points and discuss especially the two paragraphs referring to the Jews which were so widely publicized in the press.

The declaration begins by pointing out that the conditions of modern life are drawing all people closer together into one world. In her task of fostering unity and love among all individuals and nations, the Church turns her attention in this document especially to what men have in common and what draws them to fellowship. They are all the children of God, destined by Him to dwell over the face of the earth. The final goal of all is God. His providence and saving design embrace all mankind.

From the various religions men expect answers, today as in the past, to the great riddles of human existence: What is the meaning and purpose of life? What is moral good? Which is the road to happiness? Whence have we come and whither are we going? Men generally acknowledge the existence of a Supreme Being and this recognition penetrates their lives with a deep religious sense.

Religions in societies with an advanced culture have endeavored to answer man's deep questionings by means of more refined concepts and a more developed language. In Hinduism men seek an escape from the anguish of the human condition through ascetical practices, profound meditation and a flight to God with trust and love. Buddhism, in its various forms, teaches a way by which men may be able either to achieve a state of perfect liberation or attain, by their own efforts or through divine aid, supreme liberation. Other religions propose various "ways," comprising rules of life, teachings and sacred rites.

"The Catholic Church," says the declaration, "rejects nothing that is true and holy in these religions. She regards with sincere reverence those ways of conduct and of life, those precepts and teachings which, though differing in many aspects from the ones she holds and sets forth, nonetheless often reflect a ray of that Truth which enlightens all men." Indeed the Church proclaims Christ as "the way, the truth, and the life" (Jn. 14:6), in whom men may find the fullness of spiritual life, in whom God has reconciled all creatures to Himself.

Consequently the Church encourages her members to engage in dialogue and collaboration with the followers of other religions, conducted with prudence, love and in witness to the Christian faith and life. Why? So that her members may recognize, preserve and promote the good things, moral and spiritual, as well as the socio-cultural values found among these people.

The Church looks with esteem also upon the Moslems. They worship the one God, the Creator of heaven and earth, who has spoken to men. They submit wholeheartedly to His inscrutable decrees just as Abraham, with whom the faith of Islam likes to link itself, submitted to God. Though Moslems do not acknowledge Christ as God, they revere Him as a prophet. They also honor His virgin mother, Mary, and at times even call on her with devotion. They likewise hold the moral life in high esteem and worship God particularly through prayer, fasting and almsgiving.

The Council acknowledges that in the course of centuries numerous quarrels and wars occurred between Moslems and Christians. It urges all, however, to forget the past and to work sincerely for mutual understanding and for the benefit of all mankind to promote social justice, moral welfare, peace and freedom.

Our Debt to Israel

Turning its attention to Israel, the Council states that as it studies the mystery of the Church, it recalls the strong bonds which spiritually bind the people of the New Covenant to Abraham's stock.

The Church acknowledges that, according to God's design, the beginnings of her faith are found among the patriarchs, Moses and the prophets. She recognizes that the salvation of the Church is mysteriously prefigured by the chosen people's exodus from the bondage of Egypt.

Hence the Church will always remember that she received the revelation of the Old Testament through the people with whom God in His ineffable mercy and wisdom concluded the Ancient Covenant. She is clearly conscious also that she draws nourishment from the root of the well-cultivated olive tree onto which have been grafted the wild shoots, the Gentiles. Indeed the Church professes that, by His death on Calvary, Jesus reconciled Jews and Gentiles, making both one in Himself.

Vivid in her memory are the words of the Apostle Paul concerning his kinsmen: "Theirs is the sonship and the glory and the covenants and the worship and the promises; theirs are the fathers and from them is the Christ according to the flesh" (Rom. 9:4-5). The Church remembers also that the Apostles, her mainstay and pillars, as well as most of the early disciples who proclaimed Christ's good tidings to the world, stem from the people of Israel.

As Holy Writ testifies, Jerusalem did not unfortunately recognize the time of her visitation, nor did many of the Jews accept the Gospel. Indeed most opposed its message and its proclamation. "Nevertheless," says the declaration, "God holds the Jews most dear for the sake of their Fathers; He does not repent of the gifts He makes or of the calls He issues—such is the witness of the Apostle."

Along with the prophets and the Apostle Paul, the Church awaits the day, known only to God, when all peoples will address the Lord in a single voice and "serve him shoulder to shoulder" (Soph. 3:9). Because the spiritual heritage common to Christians and Jews is so great, the Council wishes to foster mutual understanding and respect, which are the fruit of biblical and theological studies and of fraternal dialogues.

The Deicide Issue

The document then comes to the most sensitive issue of all: the question of the guilt of the Jewish people for the death of Christ.

The original version, approved by the Council with a 1,770 to 180 vote on November 20, 1964, read as follows: "This Synod, in her rejection of injustice of whatever kind and wherever inflicted upon men, remains mindful of that common patrimony and so deplores, indeed condemns, hatred and persecution of Jews, whether they arose in former or in our own days.

"May all, then, see to it that in cathechetical work or in preaching they do not teach anything that could give rise to hatred or contempt of Jews in the hearts of Christians. May they never present the Jewish people as one rejected, cursed, or guilty of deicide. All that happened to Christ in His passion can in no way be attributed to the whole people then alive, much less to the people of today."

The sentence which many Jews not only eagerly welcomed but deemed essential for a complete and unqualified repudiation of anti-Semitism and its alleged chief source was: "May they never present the Jewish people as one rejected, cursed or guilty of deicide." As a number of the votes favoring the substance of the declaration contained suggestions for slight changes in the wording, the voting on the final draft was delayed until the next and last session of the Council. Then the two paragraphs previously quoted were revised to read as follows:

"True, the Jewish authorities and those who followed their lead pressed for the death of Christ; still, what happened in His passion cannot be charged against all the Jews, without distinction, then alive, nor against the Jews of today. Although the Church is the new people of God, the Jews should not be presented as rejected or accursed by God, as if this followed from the holy Scriptures. All should see to it, then, that in catechtecial work or in the preaching of the word of God they do not teach anything that does not conform to the truth of the Gospel and the spirit of Christ.

"Furthermore, in her rejection of every persecution against any man, the Church, mindful of the patrimony she shares with the Jews and moved not by political reasons but by the Gospel's spiritual love, decries hatred, persecutions, displays of anti-Semitism, directed against Jews at any time and by anyone."

In the final draft, the phrase "guilty of deicide" was omitted. Does this weaken the declaration's repudiation of anti-Semitism? There is no evidence that it does. That phrase, as Auxiliary Bishop

Levin of San Antonio had declared at the 1964 session, should be torn completely out of the Christian vocabulary. How can this be accomplished most effectively? By giving the ugly phrase a permanent dwelling place in the official declaration, where it would be regurgitated in the mind of every reader, or by exorcising it completely from the text? The Council decided that the latter was the more effective.

Here it is important to note that the declaration was addressed to Catholics and not to Jews. Hence the Council was concerned primarily with inculcating into the minds of Catholics the duty of eradicating every form of anti-Semitism not with ministering to the nuances of Jewish sensitivity. This is substantially the point made also by two experts at the Council.

In discussing this matter with Jewish representatives in Rome, Father Thomas Stransky, C.S.P., a member of the Secretariat for Promoting Christian Unity, said: "This declaration, you have to remember, is addressed to Catholics. This is Catholic Church business. For those within the Church the final text is better and more effective than the previous version." Such too is the view of Father Felix Morlion of Pro Deo University in Rome, who headed the study group working closely with the American Jewish Committee. "The first approved text," he said, "had more regard for the sensitiveness of the Jewish people, but it did not produce the necessary clearness in the minds of Christians. In this sense, it was less effective even to the very cause of the Jewish people."

Unqualified Condemnation of Anti-Semitism

Their judgment was strikingly confirmed by the findings of the Interreligious Affairs Department of the American Jewish Committee, of which Rabbi Marc H. Tannenbaum is the national director. Speaking on a nationwide NBC-TV news program Rabbi Tannenbaum said: "A survey of the religious press of the United States, Europe and Latin America has revealed that the overwhelming majority of the Catholic community has accepted the Vatican Council Declaration as a clear and unambiguous mandate to repudiate anti-Semitism and adjure the use of the ancient charge of collective Jewish guilt in the death of Jesus and allied teachings of contempt. The statement is regarded as an effort to create a new basis for relationships through dialogue and studies which will in turn lead to mutual knowledge and trust. In the perspective of 1900 years of Jewish-Christian relations, that represents an enormous step forward."

After the paragraphs discussed, the declaration proceeds to point out that Jesus underwent His passion and death voluntarily, because of the sins of men and out of infinite love, in order that all may attain salvation. Consequently the burden of the Church's preaching was to proclaim the cross of Christ as the symbol of God's all-embracing love and as the source from which every grace flows.

Furthermore, if we fail to respect the dignity of any man, created as he is in the image of God, we cannot truly call on God, the Father of all. Our relations to God the Father and to all our fellow men, our brothers under God, are so linked together that Scripture says: "He who does not love does not know God" (1 Jn. 4:8). Consequently there is no basis for discrimination between man and man or people and people so far as their human dignity and the rights flowing from it are concerned.

Accordingly the Church reproves, as alien to the mind and spirit of our Lord, any discrimination against men or harassment of them because of their race, color, condition of life or religion. Following in the footsteps of Christ and of the Apostles, the Council earnestly exhorts the Christian faithful to "maintain good fellowship among the nations" (1 Pet. 2:12) and to live in peace with all men, so that they may truly be sons of the Father who is in heaven.

XIII.

THE CHURCH IN THE
MODERN WORLD

ONE of the longest documents issued by the Second Vatican Council is the *Pastoral Constitution on the Church in the Modern World*. The massive 30,000-word, 84-page statement covers a wide range of topics and is addressed not only to Catholics but also to all other people. The first part, "The Church and Man's Calling," shows how man's vocation is realized in the community of life of the human family, in the midst of which the Church is present. The second part, "Some Problems of Special Urgency," comes to grips with such vital issues as war and peace, marriage and the family, the population explosion, poverty and economic, social and political problems.

This schema provoked some of the warmest debate of the entire Council. Even after extensive re-writing done between the third and the fourth sessions, the document was criticized on several grounds; its style was termed faulty and its clarity was questioned. So too was its tone. Some Council Fathers contended it was too naturalistic and not sufficiently centered on Christ. Others considered it too intellectualistic, while still others found it "too Western" in orientation.

A large part of the subject matter in the first part of the schema is treated in the light of the principles formulated in the *Constitution on the Church* and along the lines of social doctrine long identified with the Church. The discussion of atheism and materialism led some members to try to incorporate into the text a new condemnation of communism. The motion was rejected by the majority, however, on the grounds that this Council was essentially pastoral and the Church's present condemnation was sufficiently well-known.

The entire document represents a tremendous and sustained effort of the Council Fathers to carry out the pastoral objectives of the Council and to increase the relevance of the Church's teachings to the urgent needs of a world which had changed so radically since the previous Vatican Council was held nearly a century ago. Space will permit the presentation only of the chief highlights of this important document.

In its introductory statement the document depicts the situation of men in the modern world. It portrays the amazing scientific and technological developments triggered by the intelligence and creative energies of man. Though these have produced an un- paralled amount of wealth, resources and economic power, yet a huge proportion of the world's citizens are still tormented by hun- ger and poverty, while vast numbers suffer from complete illiteracy. Despite the fact that the world has a vivid awareness of its unity, it is divided into opposing camps by conflicting political, economic, racial and ideological differences.

These differences, backed by nuclear bombs, threaten the very existence of the entire human family. The Council points out that, beneath all the changes effected by modern science and technology, there are many realities which do not change and which have their ultimate foundation in Christ, who is the same yesterday and today and forever. Hence the Council wishes to bring the light of Christ's teachings to help man solve the problems which weigh so heavily upon him today.

The Dignity of Man

The document then devotes its first chapter to an exposition of the dignity of the human person. Through his bodily composition man gathers to himself the elements of the material world and thus, through him, they raise their voices in praise of the Creator. Man's body is vivified by a spiritual soul, which renders man into the image of God and constitutes the title to his moral grandeur and his everlasting life.

In the mysterious depths of conscience man detects a law which he does not impose upon himself, but which thunders forth its demand for obedience. In compliance with that demand man achieves his dignity and advances in virtue and holiness of life. On the other hand, the individual who turns a deaf ear to the voice of conscience degrades himself and becomes practically blind as a consequence of habitual sin.

From the very circumstance of his origin, man is dependent on God and is invited to converse with Him. Man would not exist were he not created by God's love and constantly preserved by it. Unless he freely acknowledges that love and responds to it, he cannot advance in moral character or holiness of life. It is in the failure to recognize the vital link intimately connecting man with God that the error and malice of atheism lie.

Pressing upon the Christian is the duty to battle against the manifold evils of the world at the cost of suffering and even of death. Linked with the paschal mystery and patterned on the dying Christ, he will hasten forward to resurrection in the strength which comes from hope. This holds true not only for Christians but also for all men of good will, in whose hearts grace works in an unseen manner.

Since our divine Redeemer died for all men, and since the ultimate vocation of man is in fact one, we ought to believe that, in a manner known only to God, the Holy Spirit offers to every man the possibility of being associated with the paschal mystery. Through Christ and in Christ, the riddles of sorrow and death become meaningful but, apart from Christ and His Gospel, they overwhelm us. By His resurrection Christ destroyed the power of death, and He lavishes life upon us so that as His sons we can cry out, "Abba, Father!"

The Community of Mankind

The modern world, the Council points out, is characterized by the increasing dependence of men on one another, due chiefly to modern technical advances. Brotherly dialogue among them does not, however, reach its perfection on the level of technical progress but on the deeper level of interpersonal relationships. These demand mutual respect for the total spiritual dignity of the human person.

It is here that Christian revelation makes a significant contribution: it promotes a communion between persons and leads them to a deeper understanding of the laws of social life which God has written into man's moral and spiritual nature. With fatherly solicitude for all, God has willed that all men should constitute one family and treat one another in a spirit of brotherhood. From one man God created the whole human race and arranged for them to "live all over the face of the earth" (Acts 17:26).

Furthermore, God has given all men a common destiny: union with Him in everlasting love. Love for God is the first and greatest commandment, and the second, which cannot be separated from the first, is that we love one another. "Love, therefore," as St. Paul tells us, "is the fulfillment of the Law" (Rom. 13:10). At the Last Supper the Lord Jesus prayed "that all may be one . . . as we are one" (Jn. 17:21–22). He thus opened up vistas long closed to human reason because He implied a likeness between the union of the three divine Persons and the unity of God's children in truth and love. This likeness reveals that man cannot fully find himself except in loving union with others.

Love for neighbor obliges us therefore to oppose with all our strength evils such as genocide, abortion, euthanasia; whatever violates the integrity of the human person such as mutilation, torments inflicted on body or mind and attempts to coerce the human will through "brainwashing"; subhuman living conditions, arbitrary imprisonment, deportation, slavery and prostitution; shameful working conditions where men are treated as mere tools for profit rather than as free and responsible persons.

Such evils poison human society. They cause more harm to those who inflict them than to those who suffer them. Respect for the basic rights of the human person demands that we oppose every type of discrimination, whether social or cultural, whether based on sex, race, color, social conditions, language or religion. It should prompt us to struggle for socal justice and for fair wages for all workers, whether skilled or unskilled.

It has pleased God, points out the Council, to sanctify men and save them not merely as individuals but by making them into a single people. From the beginning of salvation history, God has chosen men not just as individuals but as members of a certain community. This communitarian character is continued, developed and consummated in the mission of Christ. The Word became incarnate to share in human fellowship. It was not beneath Christ's dignity to attend the wedding at Cana, to visit the home of Zachaeus and to eat with publicans and sinners.

In his preaching Jesus taught His followers to love not only one another but also their enemies and to do good to them. On Calvary's Cross He suffered tortures and died for the redemption of all men. "Greater love than this no one has, that one lay down his life for his friends" (Jn. 15:13). Jesus commanded His disciples to proclaim to all peoples the Gospel's message that the human race was to become the Family of God, in which the fullness of the Law would be love.

He founded the Church to perpetuate that message so that all its members would render service to one another according to their different gifts. This solidarity must be steadily increased until that day when it will be brought to perfection. Then, saved by grace, men will offer flawless glory to God as a family of God and of Christ their elder Brother.

Man's Activity Throughout the World

The constitution observes that today man through science and technology has extended his mastery over nearly the whole of nature and continues to do so. Far from deeming the works produced by man's talent and energy to be in opposition to God, Christians regard them as a sign of God's grace and the flowering of His own mysterious design. The greater man's power becomes, the farther his individual and community responsibilities extend. Hence the norm of human activity is this: that in accord with the divine plan it harmonizes with the genuine good of the race and enables men as individuals and as members of society to pursue their total vocation and to fulfill it.

If research in any field of knowledge is carried out in a truly scientific manner and in accordance with moral norms, it never conflicts with the Christian faith. Why? Because the truths of science and those of faith stem from the same ultimate source: the mind of the Creator. He is the author not only of both, but also of the mind of man, by which these truths are deciphered from the vast book of nature and from the revealed word of God in holy Scripture.

The latter teaches mankind what the experience of the ages confirms: that while human progress brings great advantages to man, it brings also strong temptations. When the order of values is jumbled and individuals are concerned only with their own interests, the world ceases to be a place of true brotherhood. In our own day man's nuclear weapons threaten to destroy the race itself. If anyone wants to know how this threat can be removed, Christians will tell him that all human activity, tainted by man's pride and greed, must be purified and perfected by the power of Christ's cross and resurrection.

To those who believe in divine love, God gives assurance that the way of love lies open to men and that the effort to establish a universal brotherhood is not a hopeless one. He cautions them that this charity is not something to be reserved for important matters, but must be pursued chiefly in the humdrum routine of our daily lives.

The Lord Jesus left behind a source of strength for life's journey in that sacrament of faith, where natural elements refined by man are gloriously changed into His body and blood, providing a meal of brotherly solidarity and a foretaste of the heavenly banquet. After we have obeyed the Lord and cultivated in our daily lives the habits of kindness, compassion, brotherhood and mutual love, we shall find them again, but freed of stain, burnished and transfigured, when Jesus hands over to the Father "a Kingdom eternal and universal, a Kingdom of truth and love, of holiness and grace, of justice, love and peace." On this earth that kingdom is already present in mystery. When the Lord returns it will be brought into full flower.

The Church's Role in the Modern World

All that the Council has said previously in this document about the dignity of man, the human community and the profound meaning of human activity lays the foundation for the relationship between the Church and the world, and provides the basis for the dialogue between them. Then the Council focuses its attention on this same Church as she exists in the world, living and acting with it.

At once a visible association and a spiritual community, the Church goes forward with humanity and experiences the same earthly lot which the world does. She serves as a leaven and as a kind of soul for human society as it is to be renewed in Christ and transformed into God's family. The earthly and the heavenly city penetrate each other. Pursuing the saving purpose entrusted to her, the Church not only communicates divine life to men but in some way casts the reflected light of that life over the whole earth.

How? By her healing and elevating impact on the dignity of the person, by strengthening the seams of human society and imbuing the everyday activity of men with a deeper meaning and importance. Through her individual members and her whole community, the Church is confident she can contribute greatly toward making the family of man and its history more human.

Since it has been entrusted to the Church to reveal the mystery of God, who is the ultimate goal of man, she unfolds to man the meaning of his own existence and the innermost truth about himself. The Church is conscious that only God meets the deepest yearnings of the human heart which is never fully satisfied with the transient pleasures of this world. Through the incarnation Christ was able to sanctify, by His cross and resurrection, the whole of man, body and soul, as well as the whole of nature created by God for man's use.

The Council exhorts Christians to fulfill their earthly duties conscientiously and in the spirit of the Gospel. They err who think that religion consists only in formal acts of worship and in the fulfillment of certain moral obligations, leaving them free to plunge into secular affairs in such a way as to imply that these are quite divorced from the religious life. Such a split between the Christian faith, which many profess, and their daily lives is one of the serious errors of our day.

The Christian who neglects his mundane duties, neglects his duties toward his neighbor and even God and endangers his eternal salvation. Secular duties and activities belong properly, although not exclusively, to laymen. The latter should realize that it is generally the function of their enlightened Christian conscience to see that the divine law is woven into the life of the earthly city. Since laymen are called to play active roles in the whole life of the Church, they are obliged not only to penetrate the world with a Christian spirit but also to be witnesses for Christ in the midst of human society.

The Church encourages her children to promote the welfare of society in its economic, social and political dimensions, both nationally and internationally. While aiding the world and receiving many benefits from it, the Church has a single objective: that God's kingdom may come, and that the salvation of the whole human race may come to pass. Every benefit and service which the People of God during their earthly pilgrimage can offer to the human family stems from the fact that the Church is the universal sacrament of salvation, simultaneously manifesting and exercising the mystery of God's love for man.

The Son of God became man so that He might save all men and sum up all things in Himself. The Lord Jesus is the goal of human history, the focal point of the longings of history and of civilization, the center of the human race, the joy of every heart and the answer to its eager hopes and yearnings. Jesus is our crucified Redeemer, raised by the Father from the dead, lifted on high and stationed at His right hand, where He is the judge of the living and the dead. Vivified by His Spirit and united with Him, we journey toward the consummation of human history, which fully squares with the counsel of God's love: "To re-establish all things in Christ, both those in the heavens and those on the earth" (Eph. 11:10).

Part Two: Problems of Special Urgency

Having discussed the dignity of the human person and the work which men have been destined to undertake in the world, both as individuals and as members of society, the Council turns its attention to a number of urgent needs which characterize our age and which go to the roots of the human race: marriage and the family, human progress, life in its economic, social and political dimensions, the bonds between the family of nations, and peace.

Regarding marriage, the Council declares that it is divinely instituted and that the family is the bedrock of society. By presenting certain key points of the Church's teachings in a clearer light, the Council offers guidance and support to Christians and others who are striving to preserve the holiness and to foster the dignity of marriage.

Matrimony and conjugal love are ordained for the procreation and education of children and find in them their ultimate crown. Through their marriage vow man and woman become "no longer two but one flesh" (Mt. 19:6), and thus render help and service to each other. Strengthened by their mutual love, the spouses grow in holiness and perfection day by day. This intimate union and the good of the offspring require total fidelity of the spouses and an unbreakable union between them.

The Lord Jesus abundantly blessed this many-faceted love, which wells up from the fountain of divine love, and is structured on the model of His union with the Church. As God of old made Himself present to His people through a covenant of love and fidelity, so today the Saviour of men and the Spouse of the Church comes into the lives of married Christians through the sacrament of matrimony. Jesus abides with them thereafter so that just as He loved the Church and handed Himself over on her behalf, the spouses should love each other with abiding faithfulness and increasing devotion.

Conjugal Love

Far from looking upon the procreation and education of children as the only two ends of marriage, the Council recognizes the enormously important role which the conjugal act plays in nourishing and deepening the love of spouses, thus strengthening the marital bond. The rich interpersonal values stemming from the marriage relation, even when no offspring result, which have been stressed so greatly in recent years by psychologists, marriage counselors and moral theologians, are recognized and acknowledged with refreshing candor in this document. It is a far cry from the teaching of St. Augustine, which colored the thinking of many writers and theologians for centuries, that offspring alone justified the marriage act, and that its pleasures were otherwise sinful.

Speaking of the salutary, virtuous and sanctifying character of conjugal love, the Council says: "It involves the good of the whole person, and therefore can enrich the expressions of body and mind with a unique dignity, ennobling these expressions as special ingredients and signs of the friendship distinctive of marriage. This love God has judged worthy of special gifts, healing, perfecting and exalting gifts of grace and charity. Such love, merging the human with the divine, leads the spouses to a free and mutual gift of themselves, a gift providing itself by gentle affection and by deed; such love pervades the whole of their lives: indeed by its busy generosity it grows better and grows greater."

The many benefits that physicians, psychiatrists and marriage counselors depict as flowing from the normal exercise of the conjugal relation in the way of emotional tranquility, mental serenity and deeper love are frankly acknowledged in the Council's statement. Indeed it goes further by stating that the intimate expression of conjugal love merges human love with the divine and that God enriches it with "healing, perfecting and exalting gifts of grace and charity." Coming from the Church's highest magisterium, the statement takes on added significance. Indeed it is a good instance of the *aggiornamento* or updating of the Church's doctrine and practice, for which the Council was convened.

Spouses Determine the Number of Children

Marriage and conjugal love are, of course, by their nature ordained toward the procreation and education of offspring. Hence, while not rating the other purposes of marriage of less account, the couple should be ready with stout hearts to cooperate with the love of the Creator, who through them will enlarge and enrich His own family. In determining when to welcome a new offspring and how many, the spouses should consider their own health and welfare and that of the children already born, the material and spiritual conditions of the time, of the temporal society and of the Church.

While they should welcome the general guidance and the teachings of the Church, the spouses are the ones who know best the condition of their health, economic resources and capacity to beget and educate offspring and they must make the decision as to the time of pregnancy and the number of children in the light of their informed consciences. Thus the Council explicitly states in regard to such a judgment: "The parents themselves and no one else should ultimately make this judgment in the sight of God." This represents a distinct and notable development of the Church's teaching on this subject.

The Council recognizes that conditions of modern life will at times keep couples from increasing the size of their families. This will present difficulties in regard to the faithful exercise of love and the maintenance of the full intimacy of their lives. Yet with some restraint on their part and the guidance of properly qualified physicians in determining the periods of infertility, couples will solve the problem without resorting to measures disapproved by the Church.

Since the matter of deciding whether or not new methods of regulating conception can be harmonized with the norms of Catholic morality was reserved to the pope, aided by a special commission of about 60 members, the Council did not enter upon an explicit discussion of this particular question. It contents itself with pointing out that, when difficulties arise, Christians will provide on behalf of family life the necessities and helps which are suitably modern.

To this end, the Christian instincts of the faithful, the upright moral consciences of men, and the wisdom and experience of persons versed in the sacred sciences will have much to contribute. Those too who are expert in other sciences, especially the medical, biological, social and psychological, can considerably advance the welfare of marriage and the family if, by pooling their efforts, they explain more thoroughly the various conditions favoring a proper regulation of births.

The Council encourages properly trained priests to nurture the vocation of spouses, by preaching God's word, by liturgical worship, and by other spiritual aids, to conjugal and family life. Various family organizations, such as Pre-Cana and Cana Conferences and the Christian Family Movement, should try by programs of instruction and action to strengthen young people and the spouses themselves, especially those recently wed, and to train them for family, social and apostolic life.

Lastly the Council appeals directly to the spouses themselves, made in the image of the living God and enjoying the dignity of persons, to be united to each other in equal affection, harmony of mind and deeds of mutual sanctification. Thus by the sacrifices and joys of their holy vocation and through their devoted love, married people can bear witness to the mystery of love which the Lord revealed to the world by His dying and His rising up to life again.

The Proper Development of Culture

The Council points out that there are many ties between the message of salvation and human culture. In revealing Himself to His people through His incarnate Son, God spoke according to the prevailing culture. Similarly the Church, living and teaching in different centuries and cultures, has endeavored to utilize the prevalent culture to proclaim the Gospel and to carry out her liturgical life. While sent to all nations, the Church is not tied exclusively to any particular way of life, recent or ancient. Conscious of her universal mission, the Church enters into communion with various civilizations to their enrichment and her own.

Economic and Social Life

God created the earth and everything contained in it for the use of all mankind, the constitution declares. In using them man should regard the external things that he legitimately possesses not only as his own but also as common in the sense that they should be able to benefit not only himself but others as well. In other words, he should consider himself as a steward who will be called to render to God an account of the use he made of the things entrusted to him.

The right of establishing unions for working people is one of the fundamental rights of the human person. Such organizations should be able truly to represent the workers and to advance their economic welfare. Workers have the right of participating actively in these unions without risk of reprisal. In this way laborers will become increasingly conscious of their own function and responsibility and thereby will come to feel that they are partners with management in the whole economic enterprise as well as in the promotion of the common good according to their aptitudes.

When disputes arise, efforts should be made through conferences with management to secure a fair settlement. If these fail, workers have the right to strike, though ways should be sought as quickly as possible to secure a just settlement through a board of arbitrators representing both sides. Both labor and management should remember that there is a large area of common interest and the effort should constantly be made to increase that area for the welfare not only of labor and management but also for the general public.

Private ownership of external goods contributes to the expression of the personality and is necessary for the autonomy of the individual and the family. It offers incentives for carrying out one's function and responsibility and should be regarded as an extension of human freedom. The right of private ownership, however, is not opposed to the right inherent in various forms of public property. By its very nature private property has a social quality stemming from the common destination of earthly goods.

In many underdeveloped regions there are vast rural estates which are only slightly cultivated or completely idle, while the majority of people are either without land or have exceedingly little. Deprived of all security, they live as serfs with no chance of advancement or any share in either the social or political life. In such regions and countries reforms are urgently needed to increase the family income, to improve working conditions, to augment employment and to provide incentive for private initiative.

Indeed, sparsely cultivated estates should be broken up and parcels of land be distributed to those who can farm them. Educational assistance and facilities for cooperatives should be provided. Whenever the common good requires such expropriation, however, fair compensation should be made in the light of all the circumstances. By participating actively in the struggle for economic and social justice, Christians can make a valuable contribution to the prosperity of mankind and to the peace of the world.

The Life of the Political Community

In our day the increasing respect for human dignity has stimulated efforts in many countries to establish a politico-juridical order which will protect more effectively the rights of a person in public life. These include the right freely to assemble and form associations, the right to express one's religion both publicly and privately. Adequate protection of such rights will enable citizens, individually or collectively, to take an active part in the life and government of the state.

All citizens should be mindful of their right and duty to vote to promote the common good. All that is necessary for the triumph of evil in political life is for the so-called good people to remain away from the voting booths. The Council commends those who, for the advancement of the welfare of society, devote themselves to the service of the state and take on the responsibilities of public office.

In their respective fields Church and State are autonomous and independent of each other. Each in its own domain is devoted to the personal and social welfare of man. With due consideration of the circumstances of time and place, the more closely both cooperate, the more effective and far-reaching will be their service to the common good.

While living and working within the context of human history, man is conscious of an eternal destiny and of a habitation not made by human hands. Founded in the love of God, the Church is not unmindful of man's temporal needs, while ministering to his spiritual and eternal welfare. By proclaiming the truths of the Gospel she contributes to the reign of justice and charity within the borders of a nation and between nations and promotes the political freedom and responsibility of citizens.

Peace and a Community of Nations

Condemning war with its inevitable slaughter and destruction as a means of settling differences, the Council earnestly summons all Christians to cooperate with all men in securing a peace based on justice and love and in setting up the instruments to adjudicate differences between nations. Actions which conflict with the principles of the universal moral law are criminal and blind obedience cannot excuse them.

Among the most infamous of these are those designed for the systematic extermination of an entire people, nation or ethnic group. Society must condemn them as horrible and atrocious, and commend the stout-hearted courage of those who openly oppose leaders who issue such commands. No longer can mankind accept the pleas of those who say: "We only obeyed orders." To obey such orders is to share the guilt of the military commanders.

In the absence of any international agency sufficiently powerful to compel nations to settle their differences at the conference table and thus prevent war, governments cannot be denied the right to legitimate defense. The Council recognizes that modern nuclear weapons are, however, capable of inflicting massive and indiscriminate destruction upon whole nations. Hence it issues the following declaration: "Any act of war aimed indiscriminately at the destruction of extensive areas along with their population is a crime against God and man himself. It merits unequivocal and unhesitating condemnation."

What about the claims of those who assert that the stockpiling of nuclear weapons is to be approved and commended as an effective method of deterrence? While recognizing the good faith of a nation which acts on such a belief, the Council declares that the arms race with its stockpiling of nuclear weapons is not a safe way to ensure a certain and authentic peace. Instead of eliminating the causes of war, the expenditure of increasingly extravagant sums for new and more destructive weapons incurs the danger of aggravating them.

Accordingly the Council declares: "The arms race is an utterly treacherous trap for humanity, and one which ensnares the poor to an intolerable degree. It is much to be feared that if this race persists, it will eventually spawn all the lethal ruin whose path it is now making ready." The Council calls upon all men to take advantage of the present interlude to find effective means for the just settlement of disputes between nations.

International Authority Is Needed

This requires the establishment of some public authority with the power to safegard, on behalf of all, security, regard for justice and respect for rights. If nations were to divert the vast sums now spent on arms to alleviate the sufferings of the poverty-stricken and undernourished people of the underdeveloped countries, they would advance the progress of the human race and safeguard the peace of the world.

The Council recognizes the right of conscientious objection to war, and the placing of such objectors in other-than-combat service for the good of the community. It offers detailed suggestions for the establishment of an international community to eradicate the psychological, social, economic and political causes of war and strengthen peace. The Council calls upon all Catholics to cooperate with their separated brethren and with all men of good will in the struggle for justice, freedom and peace among all men and nations. By thus giving witness to Christ and His Gospel of understanding, peace and love, we shall share with others the mystery of the heavenly Father's love.